"You're a New Leader: So Now What?"

By

Dr Darryl Cross

Testimonials

"A must read for all leaders, especially emerging leaders. Practical and relevant. Dr Darryl has considered every barrier to becoming an effective leader and he offers you succinct and effective strategies to dismantle these barriers one brick at a time. Well done Dr.D"

Janice Parviainen, Lumina Learning, Global Partner, Canada, USA, France, AU, NZ

"*You're a New Leader So Now What,* by Dr Darryl Cross, is compulsory reading for any who are about to take on increased responsibilities. It's also a handy resource for those already in leadership. I say this because Dr Cross presents advice that is sensible, practical and very necessary. Leadership, as a skill, is in grave risk of extinction. The pantheon of leaders that have failed us is depressing. *You're a New Leader So Now What* will go a long way to ensuring the reader becomes a leader who is effective and respected."

Dr Tim Hawkes, former Headmaster, The King's School, Paramatta; Author, Educator and Leadership Consultant, Sydney, New South Wales, Australia

"There is no doubt that leading people is incredibly hard and is continuing to get harder in an ever-changing, fast paced world. It is also a privilege to lead and get the opportunity to shape and make a difference in people's lives. Most new leaders get thrown the keys with limited training in what it takes to be a good or even great leader. Dr Darryl's new book gives new leaders the 'how to' in an incredibly practical way using his thirty plus years as an outstanding Leadership Coach throughout Australia and other parts of the world. A great read that should be part of your toolkit on your leadership journey."

Damien Eves, Director, The Horton Program, Perth, Western Australia

i

"This book resources those who have been newly appointed to leadership. Its teaching is relevant, pithy and brilliantly accessible. It is a 'must have' for new leaders. Leadership is no easy task. It can be lonely, dispiriting, bewildering, bureaucratically mired, and hazardous to your character. Alternatively, it can also offer hope, transformation, excitement and fulfilment. This book will help you get the right outcome."

Dr Nick Hawkes, author of the book, *Deep Leadership,* Athelstone, South Australia

"As a new leader, my first team was a bit like my first car; it endured a lot of confidence and not a lot of understanding and control. The book very quickly imparts understanding in the areas you need in order to be a valuable leader."

Toby McDonald, ERP Project Manager, Shrieve Chemical Company, Houston, Texas, USA

"A very informative straightforward easy to read and follow guide on what is required to be a good leader! A must read for anyone starting out on their journey into leadership!"

Nick Psarros, Principal, Ray White Real Estate, Port Adelaide, South Australia

"I believe that there is a serious shortage of good leadership within society and across most organisations. We desperately need good leaders at ALL levels. If our planet, and our organisations are going to survive, this hugely important competency gap needs to be urgently addressed. Darryl has put together a fantastic simple and practical guide which I think should be read by any aspiring (or even current) leader. I only wish I had done this at the start of my journey, as it would have really helped!"

Stephen Dowling, Founder and Director, ETM, Moorabbin, Victoria, Australia

"Great leadership – you know it when you see it – but how do you become a great leader? What is really the difference between managing and leading and how do 'new leaders' quickly get up to the mark? This great book enables new leaders to quickly appreciate the leadership role and what practical steps they need to take to succeed. I've seen Dr Darryl Cross' work up close in a number of organisations and situations and he brings that powerful mix of professional expertise and years of 'in-field' experience to the table. Buy it. Read it. Give a copy to every aspiring leader that you know…"

Andrew Leunig, Leunig Advisory, Norwood, South Australia

"The chapters rang true for me – it's easy to recall the early days filled with trial and error, occasional head slaps and embarrassing moments. Being a leader means you still learn from your people daily – it also means you develop future leaders. The baby boomer generation focused on building great organisations, now it's time to develop future leaders. Darryl has compiled practical insights to focus your perspective and avoid pitfalls in this must read. Valuable for tenured leaders as well as future leaders."

Sue Grosziewicz, Stategic Business Coach & Advisor, Accountable for Change, Georgia, USA

"It is refreshing to find a book that has in simple effective points, the key to transforming oneself from a technician or manager to a leader. Having been through this process myself many years ago, I only wish I had such a valuable resource like this at the time. Well done Dr Darryl Cross – superb work once again!"

Stan Kontos, Executive Chairman, Star Pharmacy Group (Aust), Kent Town, South Australia

"I have worked with Darryl throughout my managerial career. Darryl's skilled coaching has allowed me to manage my time more effectively, delegate effectively and inspire my team daily and has assisted me to future-proof my business through effective planning. The biggest benefit that I have gained from Darryl, is an understanding of how to get the most from my people. I know this book will be a great resource to anyone who finds themselves newly appointed to a leadership or management role. Add the skill for this book to your arsenal and you will be unstoppable!"

Dan Murphy, Managing Director, Galway Bay Hotel, Galway Bay, Ireland

"A comprehensive set of tools and understandings about leadership and managing people effectively. It can be used in any setting. Darryl Cross provides new managers, supervisors, and leading hands with a sound base for more quickly developing their credibility and confidence as a leader. Recommended reading."

John Stock, OAM; Chair, LifeCare; Careers Consulting Professional, Adelaide, South Australia

"The quote that has always blown me away is, 'People don't care how much you know until they know how much you care'. Leadership is all about relationships and your ability to have greater connection and rapport with your people. These connections along with a great strategy achieve great results. It's not about your technical skill; it's all about your soft skills which are actually hard skills! This book by Dr Darryl Cross is all about guiding you to be the best you that you can be – a great leader and role model and someone that they all aspire to be."

Dean O'Rourke, Executive General Manager of Residential Construction, ABN Group WA, Osborne Park, Western Australia

"In a world where people must be centric to the development of your business, this book starts by giving you the tools to look at yourself as a person in a leadership role and how you influence and coach the people that report into you. This publication is an excellent guide for a leader in the business world today. Every possible situation that you are faced with as a leader, is extensively dealt with and very good practical advice and solutions are offered to help you with the challenges that lie ahead. As a leader myself, I find this book to be an excellent 'go to' reference guide."

**Timothy Hayes, Managing Director,
Hodson Bay Group, Ireland**

"So many of us have started our leadership journey with no guidance, tools or instructions. It's a wonder that often we arrive at a point where we feel overwhelmed and somewhat isolated in our new role. Fortunately, we are never too old to keep learning and Dr Darryl provides all the necessary information, tools, advice and support to help you when you first start out as a leader, or even if you have been in the leadership space for some time. Anyone who is interested in leadership should read this book; any leader who offers an employee a leadership role should give a copy of this book to their employee! Dr Darryl has provided me with the most relevant and up to date leadership advice over a number of years which has helped develop my leadership skills. I continually refer to Dr Darryl's teachings to ensure continued development. These skills will stay with you for a lifetime."

**Simone Nani, General Manager, South West
Football League, Western Australia**

"This is a comprehensive book that describes the attributes and skills that make a good leader. There are valuable insights and lessons on how to improve your skills with new approaches to leadership that will benefit both business outcomes and personal lives. Thanks Darryl for writing this book that clearly sets out the key issues that face leaders and for offering thought provoking advice that will assist in the never ending journey of self-improvement.

The leadership diagnostic tool is of great assistance and quickly enables a review of self and how one currently operates. The chapter on the coaching of others is insightful and describes how this not only contributes to others, but will assist in growing as a leader through the process of giving to others genuinely and meaningfully.

Of particular note is the chapter in dealing with difficult people. One can review one's own behavior and that of others in the organisation and provides assistance in improving these situations. There were some important understandings on how to work on this critical and at times soul destroying issue that all businesses face.

This book is a great asset and guide for those leading others and seeking more effective outcomes, while being happier and more personally fulfilled through the process. Well done."

Ennio Mercuri, Managing Director, Ennio International,
Holden Hill, South Australia

"*You're a New Leader: So Now What?* contains valuable insight on how to successfully graduate from 'technician' to 'leader & coach'. Working with Darryl since 2011, these techniques have been absolute game changers for my leadership & communication development. A must read for anyone on the leadership journey."

Tammie Lord, Finance Manager, ABN Group
Victoria, Docklands, Victoria, Australia

"Dr Darryl has years of experience dealing with and maximising the potential of leaders. At last, a book that condenses those valuable insights into a practical leadership manual. Dr Darryl helped me realise that leadership success comes down to the right skills ratio split. Despite what we think, technical skills are only about 12.5% of the equation towards success, whereas the interpersonal skills are about 87.5%.

Darryl's mantra is that the best leadership posture is one of remaining a learner. If you're a learner, then this book will never be far from your fingertips."

Rev Craig Broman, City Director Adelaide, City Bible Forum; Business Coach, South Australia

"*You're a Leader: So Now What?* is an invaluable guide for the first-time manager. It effectively covers the fundamental aspects of leadership as well as the common pitfalls that should be avoided. Dr. Cross' expertise and his passion for coaching and development give him great perspective to share with leaders at all levels.

Anne Marie Infilise, President, Quadra Chemicals, Vaudreuil-Dorion, Quebec, Canada

"Like most business leaders, I progressed into management positions due to my technical ability, work ethic and passion for the business. Little did I know my technical ability would count for little moving forwards. From there on, it was all about connecting with my staff, keeping everyone accountable, managing their (and my) emotions and creating solution focused environments to enable effective decision making. *You're a New Leader: So Now What?* covers many of the challenges I've faced throughout my journey and provides simple yet effective advice for those starting out their leadership careers."

Simon Mongan, General Manager, Homebuyers Centre, Docklands, Victoria, Australia

"Throughout this book, Darryl Cross shares unique insights about both the theory and more importantly the practice of leadership that makes a difference. It cracks the code for new leaders to set the culture, empower others, to strategically influence for outcomes while continuously reflecting on the critical importance of communication, especially listening. It's typical Darryl as it is integrated, inspires you to reflect, and become more self-aware and achieve with and through people. A must read for the new leader who is passionate about influencing both people and outcomes."

Marilyn Sleath, Director, International Education, Department for Education, South Australia

"This is the book that any new leader, and for that matter, any leader looking to enhance their capability has been waiting for. Having been a leader for over 30 years and developed scores of leaders in that time, I believe Dr.Darryl has really connected with the real challenges leaders face, but more importantly, given them a roadmap and some invaluable tools to help them on them on their journey.

Most leaders arrive having been good at their technical discipline, but with no real leadership pedigree. They are often overwhelmed by the attention they are given and the misguided expectation to be the smartest and be everyone's friend.

Dr Darryl has expertly busted these myths and offers some great insights into what you really should be doing, how it will enhance your impact and how you can develop your own truly unique leadership style."

Jason Langford-Brown, Head of Europe, Sales Shift, United Kingdom

"Every new leader MUST READ and will benefit from this complete guide on the critical leadership elements for success. If you find yourself elevated to a position of leadership and are wondering now what, then Dr Darryl Cross takes you through an easy to follow, meaningful and a succinct blueprint for the modern-day leader. Inspiration awaits!"

Jeffrey Hayres, Executive General Manager, Retail WA, ABN Group, Osborne Park, Western Australia

"*You're a New Leader: So Now What?* is an excellent and valuable resource, providing practical tips that can be readily applied and drawn upon in any leadership context. As a new Executive, I have drawn comfort from the advice it provides, and through application am continuing to build confidence and successes in leading at the next level."

Kelly Barns, Director, Governance Reform, SA Health, Adelaide, South Australia

"This book has allowed me to highlight key opportunity areas for my team leaders in developing their leadership skills. The value has been in how they feel they can improve or fine tune their skills in leadership. The workplace examples have been great to relate to as well as creating action plans out of this.

I also discovered some core skills that I have learnt, but not yet implemented, as well as exploring the areas of emotional intelligence and understanding human behaviour. We are all different and we work in a very diverse environment which makes "understanding" and "communication" top priority in our workplace maintaining efficiency and effectiveness.

Loved the read and I feel that both myself and my staff members stepping up into leadership roles will take a lot of value from this book and really strengthen the leadership team creating a great workplace culture."

Tim Davies, Kitchen Production Manager, IKEA Australia, Melbourne, Victoria, Australia

"What a great resource for any new leader! There is so much involved that you are not prepared for as you advance in your career. The topics covered touch on areas every new leader experiences. I would recommend companies provide this book along with the promotion."

JoAnn Labbie, Team Development Strategist, Cory Labbie Oganization, Georgia, USA

ix

"One of the key success factors in any organisation is the quality and impact of the leadership. People do not leave organisations, they leave leaders. This means that every leader needs to be more aware of the psychology of people. Who better to receive leadership insights than from a clinical psychologist who has worked extensively with leaders from a wide range of industries and organisational size.

Many of the insights in this book cannot be found in research papers or technical journals, they come from the school of hard knocks. Even more relevant is they have been learned from studying and coaching leaders from an in-depth psychological perspective rather than a study of organisational outcomes. It is the belief systems and resulting behaviours of the exemplary leaders that lead to best practice leadership processes and this is what has largely informed the insights in this book.

As a fellow coach of leaders and business performance, I can attest to the value that any leader will gain from reading this book. Thank you Darryl for sharing your valuable experience."

Dr Chris Mason, Chairman, Mindshop International, Melbourne, Victoria, Australia

"Dr Darryl Cross' new book *"You're a New Leader: So Now What?"* is the perfect companion for the millions of people out there with lots of leadership responsibility, but little or no actual training in how to lead well.

Can leadership be taught? Absolutely. And Dr Darryl is one of the most inspiring 'leaders of the leaders' I have met. A must read for any reader with more challenges than they would like!"

Nick Mayhew, Managing Director, Alembic Strategy Ltd, London, United Kingdom

Dedicated to Professor Peter W Sheehan AO
who epitomises all that leadership is meant to be

By the same Author:

Listen Up Now: How to Increase Growth and Profit in Business by Really Listening to Your Clients and Customers

The Dark Clouds at Work: How to Manage Depressed Staff in the Workplace Whilst Increasing Morale and Productivity

Stopping Your Self-Sabotage: Steps to Increase Self-Confidence

In Pursuit of Success and Happiness: A Practical Guide

Growing up Children: How To Get 5-12 Year Olds To Behave & Do As They're Told

Teenager Trouble-shooting: How to Stop Your Adolescent Driving You Crazy

All Available as an audio-book at:
www.DrDarryl.com

Cover design by Alexey Zgola

Published by Crossways Publishing

ISBN: 0-9806101-7-6

ISBN-13: 978-0-9806101-7-8

Disclaimer

This publication is designed to provide accurate and authoritative information with regard to the subject matter covered. It is sold with the understanding that the author is not engaged in rendering legal, accounting or financial advice of any kind. If legal advice, advice relating to mental health issues or any other professional assistance is required, the services of a competent professional in the appropriate area should be sought.

The author denies any liability for incidental or consequential damages resulting from the use of the information in this book. This book is designed to assist with generating and exploring various options for increasing leadership effectiveness. It does not make decisions for the individual, but provides a range of options to be considered. No responsibility is accepted for any liabilities resulting from the actions of any parties involved.

Contents

CHAPTER 1

Congratulations on Your New Role

You've Arrived

This is what you've wanted. You've worked for this. Maybe you've planned for this. Maybe you received some specific mentoring to get you to where you wanted to head. Maybe you did some further skill training through an external training body such as a University, Vocational College or Institute. Perhaps you did a series of in-house training courses or workshops to increase your skill and ability levels.

Above all, you've worked hard. This didn't happen by accident.

Of course too, there's the possibly that it might have been simply through hard work that you were rewarded with a promotion to your new leadership role. You didn't necessarily engage in courses or mentoring or coaching; instead, you showed that you were highly skilled, reliable, dependable, conscientious and above all, you were a nice person. And the reward was a higher role and greater responsibility.

Maybe you were internally promoted or maybe you applied for this role in another company or organisation.

Where's the Training Manual?

There is however, a strange irony in relation to your new appointment.

You have spent years acquiring your trade or profession. For example, if you're a carpenter, electrician, plumber or cabinet-maker, typically, you've undergone an apprenticeship over 4 years involving some classes at your Technical or Vocational College and then there has been the on-the-job training under the eagle eye of leading hands or experienced or senior trades people. You've worked on numerous sites on numerous jobs in a range of conditions and environments. Yes, it's been a journey. However, you're good at your trade and have proved yourself. You're so good at your trade and your skill levels are so advanced that you've now been asked to be the Leading Hand, the Foreman or the Supervisor. Maybe you decided to put your hand up for the leadership role for various reasons including increased salary or status.

Similarly, if you're an accountant, physiotherapist, engineer or architect for example, you've spent four or more years studying at a University involving theory and practicums allowing you to gain the practical experience. Maybe you studied full-time and then went into the workforce. Maybe you worked part-time in say, accounting, and then studied part-time to get your diploma or degree. After you graduated, you were fortunate enough to acquire a position and you've worked hard in that role over five years or more. You're good at what you do. The management in the business or organisation can rely on you to get things done and you get on well with other staff. Perhaps you're seen as a "team player" or a "self-starter". Clients or customers like you and you have a sound reputation.

In summary, you've trained hard, you've worked hard, been diligent and you're known for a high level of skill and ability, and no doubt, known as a "good" person. It's taken maybe five to ten years to build this reputation. You know your stuff. Then maybe for advancement and an increased salary you get selected for a higher role or perhaps you expressed an interest in such a role.

So, now you've excelled in your trade or profession, you're now rewarded by being "thrown" or promoted into a role for which you've had little or NO training. Pardon?

How does that work?

You've proven yourself as a stand-out so they push you into a role or you choose a role for which you have had no preparation or training. Ironical? Yes.

Further, an additional irony is that it might have taken you 10 years or more to get to this point of competence dealing with wood, electricity, pipes, finances, physical ailments, computers, construction or designs which was difficult enough, but now you're in charge of people. In other words, dealing with the physical or technical aspects of the job is taxing enough even after about a decade of training and work, but dealing with people is another matter. Ever tried herding cats?

Talk to any team leader, manager or executive and they will tell you that their issues are rarely about the "bricks and mortar", but instead, about the people problems and these issues are many and varied and often difficult. And to make matters worse, they are all different. A far cry from the work that you previously did where there were certain themes, patterns and ways or working that you knew brought about solid results and outcomes.

And who says that because you're good at what you do, that you're also going to be good at the people management area? Maybe you're simply a really great "technician" of sorts.

The *Harvard Business Review* (July-August, 2018) had an interesting research piece (see page 28) examining 53,035 sales representatives and managers across 214 companies in a variety of industries. In short, the best sales reps did not always make the best managers. The conclusion was that companies needed to closely evaluate whether moving their top sales performers into management roles was the correct kind of move. Instead, maybe companies ought to look to giving those top performers higher pay rather than a promotion. Why? Because some people are really good technically while some others do, in fact, have strong leadership potential. They both don't go hand in hand. In essence, the research argues for two career tracks within organisations; one for those with outstanding technical skills and one for those with sound leadership potential. And continued training needs to be given to both to help them develop further.

To top off these ironies, there is no training manual which tells you how to deal with people in a leadership role. There is no guide called "Trouble-shooting" to explain how to manage yourself as a leader as well as manage people and the different scenarios that confront any leader.

And we're supposed to be a clever country? I think not. It's the same in any part of the planet. I've seen it and witnessed it. No matter whether it's England, the USA, Canada, Ireland or various parts of Australia, it's the same. Get good at your trade, profession or vocation and you get "rewarded" with having to manage people without the necessary training.

Most new leaders simply fly by the seat of their pants. It's a case of trial and error, and the errors can be embarrassing, awkward and highly distressing. Sometimes this trial and error can have serious repercussions both career-wise as well as personally. The toll on the individual can be huge. Is it any wonder that new leaders often buckle under the weight of the new role and responsibility? Is it any wonder that new leaders make serious mistakes for which sometimes there is no recourse or no coming back? And this trial and error method takes years and years to work out; up to a decade or more.

Chapter 1 Summary
Congratulations on Your New Role

There is a strange irony in relation to your new appointment. You have spent years acquiring your trade or profession and you're good at it. You're highly skilled and experienced. You know your "stuff".

However, now you're rewarded by being thrown or promoted into a role for which you've had little or NO training. Maybe you put your hand up for the new role or maybe you were asked to step up. Regardless, you now confront a new arena in which you have little or no experience or training.

CHAPTER 2

You Need to Get the Basics Right

First Impressions Count

How long does it take to make a good **first impression**? What would you guess? I've asked that question numerous times in workshops and in the MBA Leadership class that I used to facilitate and I usually received varied responses from 1 second to 2 minutes.

There is little doubt that we make our judgments "snap" judgments.

I've read 7 seconds, I've read 10 seconds. Malcolm Gladwell in his book *"Blink"* indicates that it's about 3 seconds and backs it up with good research evidence. For example, Gladwell compares the intuitive responses of a university class rating a teaching Professor after 3 seconds of observation compared with responses following the examination of the same Professor after an extended time viewing video tapes of the Professor teaching. The result? No significant difference. The conclusion? That our intuitive first hunches are as good as our prolonged observations and evaluation.

If you're new to the organisation or business, then remember that first impressions definitely do count.

"First impressions are the most lasting"

(Proverb)

Further, Dr Judith Glaser at the 2016 International Coach Federation Australasian Conference in both her Keynote address and her subsequent workshop maintained that neurologically, it takes just 0.07 seconds for the brain to work out if someone is "like you" or "not like you".

You get the picture? If first impressions are that quick, you need to make sure that you create good first impressions.

*"You don't get a second chance to
make a good first impression"*

(Author unknown)

So, at a personal level, what does that mean for how you present? What do you need to do to make a good first impression? Do you smile, look at the person in the eye, have a firm handshake and call them by name?

You're On Before You're On

Let me ask you another question? Who is the most watched person in anyone's life? Yes, I'm aware that we watch ourselves constantly, but beyond that, who is the most watched person? If you're in a relationship, then it is your spouse or partner. If you're a child, then it is your parent or parents.

So, then who is the second most watched person in anyone's life? Who would you guess? It's the boss.

What does this mean therefore? Basically, *you're on before you're on.* As the new team leader, the new supervisor, the new leading hand, or manager, you are now being watched. Staff watch your moods, your attitude, your behaviour, how you handle yourself, what you stand for and generally, how you conduct yourself.

Can they trust you? Are you a person of integrity and honesty with sound emotional intelligence? Are you approachable and open in your communication? Do you give recognition and acknowledgement where it is due? Do you show vulnerability when necessary? Do you have a humble disposition? Are you organised and delegate appropriately? How do you cope with stress and deadlines?

On the other hand, do you play favourites, and cause clichés and silos to form? Do you play "being right", where you are prone to put people down who do not agree with you or do you criticise those (often in public) who have a different opinion. Is it a case of your way or the highway? Are you an ego where it's all about you where you take all the credit for things accomplished, but blame others when things might go wrong somehow? Do you try to get on-side with everyone and be their friend which means that you really don't lead at all? Maybe you don't do any of this all of the time, but just occasionally which is enough to send alarm bells ringing for your team or staff.

You're the boss now and people want to know how to connect to you and whether you can be trusted. Their work satisfaction and happiness as well as their work engagement depends to a very large part as to who you are and how you manage yourself. Their future and perhaps their professional growth and possible promotion may well rest in your hands.

Are they going to watch you? You bet they are!

The harsh reality though is that it is part of human survival for us to be weighing up our surrounds, and the people in it. Moment by moment we are evaluating what is going on around us, taking in information and sizing up our situation. It is human nature.

Not surprisingly, we naturally weigh up those in our vicinity because we need to know how we might respond and interact with them. We take in data constantly and our radar is constantly scanning our horizon to check how we might react and respond. We measure and note what people say, and how they say it. We evaluate what people do and how they do it. Constantly monitoring and scanning. I read recently that our brain consists of 86 billion neurons and several hundred trillion connections. Yes, we can't help our brain doing what it's supposed to do. Scan and make sense of our surrounds.

From the moment you get out of the car in car-park or the way you walk into the building or the way that you walk on-site or the way that you walk around the factory, you are being watched. At one location where I coached, staff used to tell me that they could fairly well determine what sort of day they were going to have with how the CEO drove into the car-park in the morning and how he then walked into the building.

I also coached a Managing Director who I suggested that when he walked to the toilet that he walk more slowing and look more relaxed. His staff were picking up messages that his quick walk to the toilet was a sign of things not being well or that he was stressed and "under the pump" and hence, it was probably not a good time to engage him. He was actually quite taken aback at receiving this feedback because it had never occurred to him that this behavior in this way could be interpreted in such a fashion. He was just a person who happened to move quickly in that he was highly energetic and action-oriented in style. He now tries hard to be aware of how he walks and moves in that he is more conscious that his staff make up a "story" about his attitude and state of mind in the way that he is being observed.

You're Rated on What You Do – Not What You Say

Words are cheap. Actions talk. Are you a person who walks the talk or just talks?

Do you follow up and do what you said you were going to do? Do you follow through? Do you get back to others when you say you were going to?

"Communication is more about what you do than what you say"

(Darryl Cross)

Integrity is one of the factors that staff look for in a leader and following up and doing what you say you will do is a clear sign of being authentic and the "real deal". If you can't meet the deadline that you promised or you can't deliver for some reason, then it is important to let the staff member know why and then work out another time that suits you both.

This brings me to the salient point about non-verbal behavior. How much of your communication is determined by your verbal behavior (ie., what you say, the content of your spoken word) versus the non-verbal behavior (ie., how you say it, the feeling or emotion that you portray)?

I have asked this question hundreds of times at countless seminars and workshops that I have conducted and I have had every response imaginable from 90% verbal to 10% non-verbal and vice-versa. Most people guess around the 50:50 or 60:40 mark to perhaps 75:25 (in both directions) while a few might guess 80:20 in both directions.

Most though have never really thought about it. Yet it is a critical question. You need to know the answer because communication is at the core of what we do every minute of every day (even when we are **not** talking) and as a leader, you are being judged on it.

Psychologist Albert Mehrabian has done extensive laboratory measurements on what happens when one person talks to another. Mehrabian conducted some milestone research way back in 1970 where he looked at the question of verbal and non-verbal communication [See L. Longfellow, "Body Talk," *Psychology Today*, October 1970, Vol. 4.

No. 5, P.46]. His work has largely stood the test of time although it has been challenged too.

What did he find? Verbal communication only accounted for **7%** of the impact whereas Non-verbal accounted for **93%** of the impact.

So, if you remember **10%** verbal and **90%** non-verbal, you'll be close to the mark. Even if it's not 10:90 and it's 20:80 or even 25:75, you get the message that there is a lot of communication that is non-verbal.

What's the point here? How you behave is a huge message that you're giving out to the world and those around you. How you conduct yourself speaks volumes.

It's not about Skills – it's about Communication

Originally, and in most cases, individuals are hired for their first or second jobs on the basis of their skills, technical knowledge and perhaps competence and experience. It doesn't matter if you started in a trainee role, as an apprentice or studied for a professional qualification, it was all about acquiring the necessary skills and knowledge. Over time, you gain greater confidence in your skills, you gain greater knowledge and understanding of the job, and you take on tasks of a more complex nature as you become more adept in your role, trade or profession.

Hence, for all of your education both at secondary level as well as post-secondary and tertiary education, it has all been about skill development and performance.

Now, however, you are a new leader and although it is expected that you have a high level of technical skills and knowledge, the ballpark has changed. Now, it is about managing people and communicating effectively – and as we have indicated above, this is a ballpark in which you have had no (or very little) formal training or education.

But this one thing you need to know, **you had better get good at communication**.

I remember reading a small book by John C Maxwell called *"Attitude 101"* about some research conducted by the Stanford Research Institute in the USA where they identified that business success and profit (as well as individual career success and promotion) was attributable to two main factors.   Namely, the following:

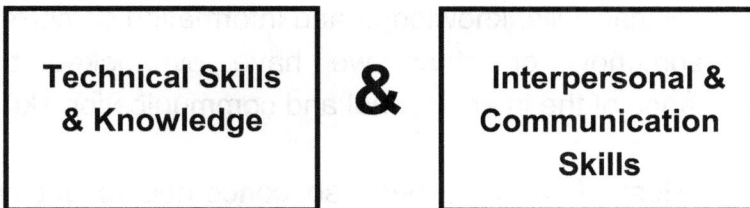

Technical Skills & Knowledge	**&**	**Interpersonal & Communication Skills**

Now, perhaps you might think that that was not surprising news. Business and career success would no doubt be due to those two factors you might say.

However, the Stanford group went a step further. They were able to attribute a percentage to each factor in relation to how much **each** contributed to success.

What would you guess was the percentage of each factor in regards to its contribution towards success?

The research findings were compelling in this regard.

Technical Skills and Knowledge attributed for only **12.5%** of the success, whereas Interpersonal and Communication Skills attributed for **87.5%**.

What does that tell you?

The cynics might say that all you really need is the "gift of the gab" and you'll be okay (and unfortunately in some cases that does happen)! However, the real message is that most of us have concentrated on getting the technical skills, knowledge and information so correct that somehow or other, we have overlooked the importance of the interpersonal and communication skills.

Most of us have been so concerned to get our "piece of paper" such as a Certificate, Diploma or Degree (including the MBA) that we haven't paid much attention to the people skills area.

In a sense, **some of us have just taken that part (ie., interpersonal & communication skills) for granted**.

Certainly, our general secondary and tertiary education sectors haven't helped either in that we have been "brain-washed" into believing that it was all about getting a good grade point average, getting qualifications and gaining knowledge. In part it is.

But in large part, there is another dimension which we haven't been taught and that's how to connect effectively with those around us and how to communicate at an effective level and how to have an impact emotionally as well as lead effectively.

So, what are those skills in the Interpersonal and Communication area that help us to be effective and to have an impact especially in the work setting? In a word it is about listening and asking good questions.

This is covered later in Chapter 9, but has also been covered in another book that I have written for leaders and managers which is titled, *"Listen Up Now: How to Increase Growth and Profit by Really Listening to Your Customers and Clients"*. It is available through www.ListenUpNow.com.au in either hardcopy, audio or kindle.

"Everything we do is communication"

(Author unknown)

Chapter 2 Summary
You Need to Get the Basics Right

First Impression Count
First impressions are quick (very quick), so you need to make sure that you create good first impressions.

You're On Before You're On
What does this mean? As the new team leader, the new supervisor, the new leading hand, or manager, you are now being closely watched by your team, how you handle yourself, what you stand for and generally, how you conduct yourself.

You're Rated on What You Do – Not What You Say
Words are cheap. Actions talk. Are you a person who walks the talk or just talks? Do you follow up and do what you say you were going to do? Do you get back to others when you say you were going to?

It's not about Skills – it's about Communication
Most of us have concentrated on getting the technical skills, knowledge and information so correct that somehow or other, we have overlooked the critical importance of interpersonal and communication skills.

CHAPTER 3

Introducing Yourself to the Group

What Do You Do After You Say Hello?

1. If you've previously been part of the group & been promoted

You were once part of the group and they were all your "mates", buddies or friends. You may well have socialised together, you've probably shared a life together, and you've interacted at the same level. Maybe you often talked about management. Maybe you all criticised management or your boss at the time. Maybe you were all critical of the way that the company or organisation was heading. Maybe you were all critical of the lack of communication and felt that you were all being kept in the dark such that you didn't trust management.

But now it's all changed. You're the boss.

No matter who you are, "they" are all going to look at you differently now whether you like it or not. Perhaps too there were others in the group who also applied for the role that you ended up winning. How do you think they might be feeling? Some will see you as "betraying" the group; others may think that now that you're the boss that they will get preferential treatment. Others will feel a sense of "loss" that it won't be same again in relation to your friendship and interaction because you have now been elevated to a different role.

What is critical here is how you manage this. **This is your first test.** Fail this and it will mean that your track ahead is going to be much more difficult than otherwise would be the case. It's going to be all about communication.

First of all, you need to speak to the group as a whole. So, what are you going to say? It is a truism that good leaders are transparent and genuine in their interactions and need to be seen as vulnerable and human just like everyone else. In that respect, it is best to be open and honest about the fact that this is going to be somewhat difficult transition into leadership for both you and them for the kinds of reasons outlined above. You need to acknowledge that this is a new role for you (as they well know) and that you will not always get it right, but importantly, you will value their feedback and their support as you find your way in this new role.

It will also be important for you, at least in a general way, to outline the vision or direction for the team in that you want it to be a team of excellence and for the team to be known as a cut above the rest. Further, it will be important to reaffirm to each of them that their own professional development and growth is something that is important to you as a leader and that you will be having discussions with each of them about how they can be their best and achieve what they would like to work towards.

It will indeed be critical then for you to set up 1:1 meetings with each of your staff to see how they feel about you being appointed to the role, how they see the unit or team, how they see their own role and where they feel they might be headed. They might have questions too to ask you about where you think the team might head or where they could head. Make sure therefore that everyone feels heard.

2. If you're an outside appointment

I heard recently that for new leaders to any group that it takes at least nine months to gain a real sense of what the business is about and to really understand the politics and the culture of the organisation.

In my own experience of changing jobs, it was more like 12 months before I really gained a sense of the organisation and where it was going, of the politics and dynamics, and of the nuances of culture. Needless to say, the critical area for me to really understand was the office politics and who liked who, and who didn't like who, the particular personalities and their strengths and foibles, the agendas that played out for individuals and for specific groups, and the niches that developed for various reasons.

All of this of course, takes time to understand. Because of the intricacies of human nature, understanding this whole dynamic is not something that can be rushed and if you do not understand the office politics, then it is probably true to say that you could well be limiting your career options. How to gain this social intelligence is probably another book in and of itself, but you need to be observant, listen intently, ask good questions, and try to use your intuitive powers to also read between the lines. Above all, don't rush in and instead, be prepared to acknowledge that it will take time to understand all the nuances and subtleties.

In this way, it would be foolish to be making changes or significant decisions in the first week or two and instead, your key role and probably for the first 30 days (at least), is to listen and ask as many questions as you can. If some members of your team try to press you for answers or decisions, simply let them know that you are in discovery mode and keen to learn before any pathways or projects can be determined.

However, on your first day in the organisation or business, or when you are introduced to your team, you will of course, need to say something by way of introduction. Needless to say, as I have intimated above, all eyes will be on you and that's from the moment you pull up in the car park or you walk up to the front door. Your comments to your new group will be similar to what I have portrayed above for individuals who have been promoted from within the group. Your opening comments are not going to be too much different except to say, that you obviously won't have to deal with issues that come from an internal promotion.

So, some vital tips to ensure that you "kick off" in the best way possible:

(1)   **Introduce yourself to everyone**. Make a point of meeting everyone in your team as well as those departments or units that interact with your team and especially the leaders within those external teams. At this point, it is simply a case of giving your name, your new role, where you are from previously, and what attracted you to the current company.

(2)   **Make it a point of learning everyone's name**. Devise your own plan to ensure that you remember everyone's name and this might mean writing it down, commandeering staff photographs, and reviewing these for homework each night so those names become entrenched. Remembering a person's name is a big leap forward in the

relationship stakes and starts to build your own personal brand too.

(3)   **Be focused on asking questions.** As has been suggested above, in these early days, it is not about you pontificating or telling or advising, and instead, it's about you discovering, exploring and investigating. This means listening. This means keeping quiet and taking it all in. Information is power. You need to understand all that you can about every aspect of the new business or organisation and you can only do this by asking questions and seeking information.

(4)   **Be positive and enthusiastic.** It may well be however, that you are anxious and feeling overwhelmed at all there is to learn and know about your new role and the business. Irrespective, you cannot afford to show this especially in these first days and as a new leader, your team will be looking to you to be positive and to eventually giving them some forward direction and pathway. This is a case therefore, of "fake it until you make it" in these early days until you start to settle down and feel more familiar in your new surroundings.

Keeping a Professional Gap

Leaders Can't Have Favourites

What can be very tricky with an internal promotion and less so if you've come externally, is to understand that you cannot afford to have best friends or close allies in the same way that you might have had when you were simply a team member. Going to lunch with the same staff members or generally hanging out with the same group for Friday night drinks for example, sends the wrong message to everyone else in the team and highlights that you may well be playing favourites. Once anyone in the team gains the notion that you may well have favourites, then you can expect office politics to rise to another level. Your leadership role will immediately be undermined and you will find it much more difficult to manage the team than otherwise would be the case.

"A man who wants to lead the orchestra must turn his back on the crowd"

(Max Lucado)

Instead, you need to understand that as a leader, you need to treat everyone impartially and equally and that as a leader you cannot have a best friend in your group. If you had a previous best buddy, then it will be critical for you to have that conversation with that individual and explain to them that although your feelings in connection with them hasn't changed, that as a leader however, you need to be seen to be doing things in a just and equitable fashion.

Leaders Can't be Friends with Everyone

New leaders often mistakenly think that they can undertake their role by being friends with everyone. There is a distinction here between being friendly and being a friend.

Being friendly means that you are warm, engaging and approachable with everyone in your team. You say "Good morning" to each one as you start the day and you're prepared to engage in brief social conversation about their weekend, their children, their family, their hobbies and generally show an interest in their lives and their activities. You're interested in them as people, but not at a deeper level.

Being a friend however, is more intense and personal and shows a deeper, more intimate connection. This "being a friend" often occurs though because the new leader wants to be liked by everyone. He or she thinks that they can be a good leader if everyone likes them and thinks well of them. Nothing is further from the truth. It's about being respected, not necessarily being liked by everyone.

If, as a leader, you are bitten by the curse of being a "People Pleaser" where you want everyone to like you, then I refer you to my other book titled, *"How to Stop Your Self-sabotage: Steps to Increase Your Self-confidence"* which is available in hardcopy, audio or kindle through:

www.HowtoStopSelfSabotage.com

"I cannot give you the formula for success, but I can give you the formula for failure, which is: Try to please everybody"

(Herbert Swope)

"Being a friend" means that you also compromise your leadership capacity. Leaders can't be friends. As a leader, you won't be able to discipline your team members (if that's necessary). You'll also find it difficult to delegate work (because you'll be imposing on your friends). You will typically find it difficult to be assertive (because then people may not like you). All this goes to say, that being a friend and being a leader do not go hand in hand. Instead, as indicated above, it is all about **being friendly**.

Beware Social Occasions

Where many new leaders fall down is on social occasions (eg., Friday night drinks at work or at the local hotel, work get-togethers to celebrate success milestones,

Christmas functions and so on) particularly where alcohol is involved (or perhaps drugs are used). Typically, the leaders "let their hair down" and they become one of the team again and possibly behave in inappropriate ways which only serves to damage their brand and reputation and undo any good work that they might have done. This is not a way to gain respect and certainly your superiors would start to question their decision to appoint you to a leadership role if you cannot manage yourself socially.

Besides, the grapevine in any organisation works extremely well and if you think that your mis-demeanours after-hours will somehow remain back at the hotel or at the function centre or wherever, then you are naïve and gravely mistaken.

Alternatively, as a new leader, you are certainly expected to join in and be present at all social get-togethers and celebrations, but you must learn to also set yourself apart. It is important that you monitor your alcohol intake, that you don't drop your guard and act inappropriately and that, in fact, you may be one of the first to leave to go home and allow your team to continue to drink and socialise.

Leadership is NOT having all the Answers

It's interesting in the coaching that I undertake with new leaders that somehow or other, there is **a myth** being perpetrated that as a leader, they should have all the answers. Somehow or other, they are supposed to know everything. If a team member, for example, comes to them with an issue or problem, somehow or other, they are supposed to come up with an answer and relatively soon.

In my experience, good leaders **do not** have all the answers, but they do have a good team around them who may well in fact, know the answers or instead, the leaders themselves know where to find the answers. Alternatively, if neither the leader nor the team member know the answer, then both decide to try to find the answer by working together.

Of course, it is expected that new leaders will be technically competent and know their skill or trade or profession well, but where is it written that they should know everything there is to know? Furthermore, in a VUCA world (Volatile, Uncertain, Complex, Ambiguous) where things are changing rapidly and where new situations are being encountered regularly such that there is no prior experience or precedent, how on earth can a leader, let alone a new leader, know everything there is to know? It's simply not possible. It's unrealistic.

The new leader needs to feel confident in themselves as a person to simply listen to the issue and ask pertinent questions and include the staff member into the conversation to see if they too, for instance, might have a possible solution or remedy to the issue or problem. If neither of these individuals can come up with a solution, then plans are set in place about who to talk to or where to go in order to access a possible solution or outcome. The leader working together with the staff member sets up an important framework for inclusiveness and respect.

A **second myth** is that somehow or other, the leader should have all the answers immediately. Where is it written that the leader should know all things straight away?

Again, this is a mistaken assumption and good leaders often need to take time to consider issues or problems and even include the various staff members again in helping to assist in finding an appropriate solution.

New leaders need to give themselves permission to discover, investigate, and take time to source various solutions often with the help of their team or a particular staff member and occasionally, to go outside the group to source an appropriate outcome.

Leadership is NOT Doing it All Yourself

There is also the notion that somehow or other the leader needs to do it all themselves and that the team success all rides on the leader's shoulders.

Of course, there is an element of truth in this, but some new leaders believe that the only way the team can be successful is if they do the work themselves, so they work back late and they work long hours to get it all done and they take on extra projects that ought to be delegated to various team members. They fix up team member's errors and they help out team members to meet deadlines that ought to have been met by the team member themselves.

"No man will make a great leader who wants to do it all himself, or get all the credit for doing it"

(Andrew Carnegie)

Not surprisingly, this new team leader will quickly become very stressed and burnout, and in the process, will be inefficient. It will also mean that they are not giving any direction or lead to their team who will be floundering with low productivity and low morale.

Instead, it is about mobilising the team, working out the strengths of each team member and encouraging and supporting the team to reach particular goals using certain strategies. More will be said about this later, but it is important for the new leader to realise quite clearly that this is not a one-person race, and in fact, it is more like a team relay where each team member relies on the other to effectively run their part of the race.

Chapter 3 Summary
Introducing Yourself to the Group

What Do you Say After You Say Hello?

1. If you've previously been part of the group and been promoted

First of all, you need to speak to the group as a whole. So, what are you going to say? There are certain topics that you need to cover. Secondly, It will be critical for you to set up 1:1 meetings with each of your staff to see how they feel about you being appointed to the role, how they see the unit or team, how they see their own role and where they feel they might be headed.

2. If you're an outside appointment

Don't rush in and instead, be prepared to acknowledge that it will take time to understand the business, the politics and all the nuances. This takes time. Observe, listen and ask lots of questions.

Keeping a Professional Gap
Leaders Can't have Favourites

Once anyone in the team gains the notion that you may well have favourites, then you can expect office politics to rise to another level and your leadership role will immediately be undermined.

Leaders Can't be Friends with Everyone

There is a distinction between being friendly and being a friend.

Beware Social Occasions

Where many new leaders fall down is on social occasions

particularly where alcohol is involved or perhaps drugs are used. Typically, the leaders "let their hair down" and they become one of the team again and behave inappropriately.

Leadership is NOT having all the Answers
There is **a myth** being perpetrated that as a leader, you should have all the answers. Good leaders do not have all the answers, but they do have a good team around them who may well in fact, know the answers or instead, the leaders themselves know where to find the answers.

A **second myth** is that somehow or other, they should have all the answers immediately. Good leaders often need to take time to consider issues or problems and even include the various staff members in helping to assist in finding an appropriate solution.

Leadership is NOT Doing it All Yourself
There is the notion that somehow or other the leader needs to do it **all** themselves and that the team success **all** rides on the leader's shoulders. Instead, it is about mobilising the team, working out the strengths of each team member and encouraging and supporting the team to reach particular goals by using certain strategies.

CHAPTER 4

What is Leadership?

How is Leadership Defined?

New leaders often come in to the role with a vague understanding how they might perform in such a position and what it is all about. As intimated above in earlier chapters, they probably have had no experience in leading except perhaps in a local sports team or on a committee of some sort. They may have attended the occasional talk or presentation on leadership, but generally speaking, they certainly have not had any formal training in what leadership really is and how to perform effectively.

Furthermore, leadership has been defined in numerous ways and sometimes it depends on who you might talk to as to how leadership might be perceived. It is probably true to say however, that in this day and age, the old-style autocratic or dictatorial form of leadership or being a benevolent dictator has given way to a more collaborative, democratic style of leadership.

Some of the more pertinent definitions of leadership that might be helpful for a new leader are given below:

"The legitimate use of power to achieve outcomes on behalf of a group of people"
(Jock Cameron, National Student Leadership Forum, Parliament House, Canberra, 20th Sept 2012)

"A leader is best when people barely know he exists, when his work is done, his aim fulfilled, they will say: We did it ourselves"
(Lao Tze; 6th Century BC, philosopher of Ancient China)

"Leadership is not defined by the exercise of power, but by the capacity to increase the sense of power among those led. The most essential work of the leader is to create more leaders"
(Follett, MP. *The Creative Experience*, NY; Longmans Green, 1924, page 3)

"A leader...is like a shepherd. He stays behind the flock, letting the most nimble go out ahead, whereupon the others follow, not realizing that all

along they are being directed from behind"
(Nelson Mandella, South African anti-apartheid
revolutionary, political leader, and
philanthropist, 1918-2013)

"Leadership is the art of getting someone else to do something you want done because he wants to do it"
(Dwight D. Eisenhower, 34th President of the United
States, 1890-1969)

"As we look ahead into the next century, leaders will be those who empower others"
(Bill Gates, American business magnate,
author, investor, philanthropist,
and co-founder of the Microsoft Corporation,1955-)

"A good leader is a person who takes a little more than his share of the blame and a little less than his share of the credit"
(John Maxwell, American author, speaker, and pastor,
1947-)

"Become the kind of leader that people would follow voluntarily; even if you had no title or position"
(Brian Tracy, Canadian-American motivational public
speaker and self-development author, 1944-)

"Average leaders raise the bar on themselves; good leaders raise the bar for others; great leaders inspire others to raise their own bar"
(Orrin Woodward, entrepreneur and author, 1967-)

"Outstanding leaders go out of their way to boost the self-esteem of their personnel. If people believe in themselves, it's amazing what they can accomplish"

(Sam Walton, American businessman and entrepreneur, 1918-1992)

"If your actions inspire others to dream more, learn more, do more and become more, you are a leader"

(John Quincy Adams, 6th President of the United States, 1767-1848)

So, what is the theme running through these quotes? Can you pick it? There might be more than one theme, but what is a predominant theme?

The over-riding theme here is that leadership is about growing others, developing others, boosting others, and empowering others. Leadership is about getting out of the way and encouraging team members to stand up and develop themselves perhaps in ways that they never would have imagined.

---

*"People remember not what you did,
but how you made them feel"*

(Darryl Cross)

Leadership Fails

Typically, leaders who fail at building support from their followers do so in a number of ways. Don't fall into these traps.

1. There are the **autocrats or dictators** who are typically ruled by their own need for power or control where they use a megaphone to blast a point of view without making anyone around them any smarter and if anything, cause their followers to withdraw and hibernate. Occasionally, they also play favourites with some of their followers and in turn, create cliques. They can be termed "bullies" or "tanks" in that their message is simple – they count and you don't – their opinion is right and yours isn't.

"Don't blow off another's candle for it won't make yours shine brighter"

(Jaachynma N E Agu)

---

2. There are the **egos where they are self-centered** and so concerned about themselves and how they look that it is indeed all about them. They may well take the credit for the work done by others and then blame others if it does go wrong. They do things for their own ends and maybe take short-cuts to achieve their own purposes. These leaders lack any kind of emotional intelligence

and are normally self-centered perhaps to a point of being narcissistic in terms of their own self-importance.

3. There are the **'abdicrats'** where they allow the free flow of democracy in such a way that it becomes almost an anarchy of misalignment. Generally speaking, in an endeavor to please or because of their own lack of confidence, they tend to go overboard to gain consensus and not surprisingly, the team loses its way without any clear direction. Sometimes too, they are just past caring (for various reasons) or have given up and the ship becomes aimless without any rudder or guidance.

4. There are the **control freaks** or micro-managers who closely monitor and critique the work of their staff. They can be over-powering in their management style and most people feel suffocated by them. This management style may be due to an over-inflated ego ("My way is best" or "My way is right") or due to a case of perfectionism, both of which are debilitating to those who work for them.

5. On the other hand, there are the **indecisive managers** who simply don't make decisions or don't provide direction where it appears that there is a lack of control, with constantly changing priorities, moving deadlines and an absence of focus. These individuals are often afraid to make mistakes or afraid to take risks (of any kind). Needless to say, staff frequently feel lost, powerless and frustrated.

6. There are the **time poor managers** who never have enough time and who spread themselves too thinly across their role. Often, they either don't have enough resources or they don't delegate effectively believing that they need to do it all themselves or be across everything in miniscule detail.

7. There are the **lack of detail managers** who give their direct reports the big picture, but who have not thought through the detail and leave too much open to interpretation. This leaves staff floundering and sometimes means that staff start to question their own self-confidence since they are not able to grasp the project or task at a practical or realistic level.

8. Finally, there are the **impulsive managers** who tend to make decisions quickly without considering the consequences or thinking things through. Not surprisingly, projects can become unstuck very quickly and become messy. This management style is unnerving to staff who are cautious and who don't trust the manager which means that morale is often low and employees feel insecure and uncertain.

Instead, leadership is a paradox of power in that it is top-down, but interactive, command-and-control, but participatory. It is a combination of leading from the front, while at the same time supporting from the rear. Yes, it might be difficult to find this line as a new leader, but the emphasis is not on you, but you encouraging and growing those around you.

There is a term for this form of leadership, it's called **transformational leadership**.

Leadership that Transforms Followers

Professor Bruce Avolio in his 2011 book titled, *"Full Range Leadership Development"* highlights the notion that the core of effective leadership is about **trust** and transformational leadership is one prime way to achieve that trust. Without it, leadership is non-existent. Let's explain that further.

In Avolio's model, there are two main components to this model; *Transactional leadership* as well as *Transformational leadership*.

As a new leader, you no doubt will focus first on the "transaction" part with a view to moving across more into the "transformational" part as you gain greater confidence and experience. Transformational leadership is what you would aspire to. So, let's briefly expand those terms.

Transactional leadership is about transactions ie., getting the roles and expectations clear, having job descriptions that adequately portray the job, setting the lines of authority and responsibility, and getting the structure right within the team. Furthermore, this would also involve setting team objectives and action plans and having performance indicators to monitor progress. First and foremost though, would be the vision and mission for the team. What does success look like in the future? What do we want to achieve? The vision is like a guiding star. Mission is about purpose. Why do we exist? What do we do? Who do we do it for? Where is the team headed? How does it intend to get there?

Without the transactional base, expectations are often unclear, direction is ill-defined, and the goals you are working toward are too ambiguous.

So, getting the transactions right consistently, in what we have labelled transactional leadership, is essential to becoming an effective leader, and having an effective team. Working off this as a solid base, the leader then turns to the transformational aspect of leadership.

Transformational leadership involves the process whereby leaders develop followers into leaders. This is a conscious goal; the leader has a development plan in her or his head about each follower or has worked out the plan in conjunction with the team member.

Such a plan might involve training and development or coaching and mentoring as well as holding the team member to account for reaching their goals and showing courage where necessary to reach those goals. It might even mean rewarding the staff member for going beyond what was originally indicated or for showing initiative or for being innovative for example.

> *"Before you are a leader, success is all about growing yourself. When you become a leader, success is all about growing others"*
>
> (Jack Welch)

Such leaders stimulate challenge, as opposed to suppressing it when it arises. They work to leave behind a team, an organisation, community or even society that is better positioned to succeed than when they first began their work. They are moral agents who focus themselves and their followers on achieving higher-level missions and purposes. The higher levels of identification result in higher levels of commitment, trust, loyalty, and performance.

If you as a new leader **honour all your various transactions with people, over time they come to trust you**; it is these higher levels of trust (versus straight compliance) that transformational leadership uses as its base for being able to achieve exemplary performance according to Avolio. In practice, this seems to work well.

Leadership is about Relationships

In essence, leadership is a relationship. As JM Kouzes and BZ Posner say in their 2002 book, *Leadership Challenge, "It's a relationship between those who aspire to lead and those who choose to follow"* (page 20).

Sometimes the relationship is one to one. Sometimes, it is one to many. Irrespective of the number, leaders must master the dynamics of this relationship. Leadership is an influence process.

"Leadership is not about titles, positions, or flow charts. It is about one life influencing another."

(John C Maxwell)

At any time you're trying to influence the behavior of someone toward a goal, you're engaging in leadership. This is so no matter whether you're a politician, a CEO, a parent, a teacher, a sports coach or a minister of religion.

Ken Blanchard asserts that leadership is about moving people from dependence to independence in pursuit of a goal. However, he considers that there are some prime requisites here. First, leadership is about going somewhere. If you don't know where you're going, your leadership doesn't matter (ie., transactional leadership). Second, it's about implementation. Certainly leaders need to give their people vision and direction, but they also need to work to get their people to move closer to their destination.

Finally, it is about serving and supporting (ie., transformational leadership). In this way, leaders serve their people by guiding and cheerleading them as their needs require.

"People don't care what you know until they know that you care."

(Author unknown)

Positive Leadership

Everyone likes to think that their leadership can be positive and much has been written on leadership and what leads to successful leadership. In fact, there are more than 70,000 books on leadership in print (and rising).

However, the Positive Leadership model proposed by Professor Kim Cameron from the University of Michigan is distinctive because **it is based entirely on validated empirical research**. Hence, it is worth taking time to consider what this model says. He has written numerous books, but you may like to read *Positive Leadership* published by Berrett-Koehler Publishers in 2012.

In short, there are four components to his model (Positive Climate; Positive Relationships; Positive Communication; and Positive Meaning). They are all defined below. Remember that every aspect of this model is based upon significant research over decades.

Components	Explanation	Key Activities
1. Positive Climate	Creating a positive climate is resisting the tendency to concentrate primarily on the negative, threatening or problematic and instead, emphasise positive phenomena by turning problems into opportunities. Research shows a significantly higher performance at work when a positive climate exists.	1. Modelling and fostering compassion 2. Encouraging collective forgiveness 3. Encouraging expressions of gratitude (visits, letters, cards)
2. Positive Relationships	This is more than people just getting along or avoiding toxicity. Instead, it is enabling positive relationships at work which impacts not only their emotional and physiological health as well as life expectancy, but positively enhances the performance in teams.	1. Assisting staff to contribute to the benefit of others rather than merely receive support 2. Network with people who are positive energisers rather than

		energy vampires 3. Helping staff become aware of their strengths
3. Positive Communication	This is about using affirmative and supportive language instead of negative or critical language. Research showed that the single most important factor in predicting organisational performance, which was twice as powerful as any other factor, was the ratio of positive statements in teams to negative statements.	1. Best feedback is not about targeting improvement in weaknesses, but about uncovering a person's strengths as perceived by others 2. Having crucial conversations that focus on the behavior and not the person
4. Positive Meaning	When people are pursuing a profound purpose or engaging in meaningful work, significant positive effects are produced including reductions in	1. Showing workers the effect of their work on others 2. Highlight connections

	stress, depression, turnover, absenteeism, dissatisfaction as well as increases in commitment, effort, engagement, happiness, satisfaction and a sense of fulfillment.	between what is meaningful to individuals and the benefits produced by the organisation 3. Highlight the long-term impact of the work 4. Build a sense of community by contributing towards others such as charities

Leaders Versus Managers

Is there a difference being a manager and a leader? Two sources listed below and anecdotal evidence certainly says that there are definite differences. Although it is true to say that most of the leaders that I coach would admit to fluctuating between the two, it is important to recognise where you are at any point in time. Are you leading or managing?

Mostly, as a new leader, you will be managing, and trying to get your head around that is more than enough for most new leaders. But, as we have intimated, although you might spend most of your time managing, there may be on occasions, times when you are actually in the leadership mode.

According to the 1994 article in *Management Review* by G Capowski, titled, *"Anatomy of a leader: Where are the leaders of tomorrow?"*, the different characteristics between a leader and manager were as follows:

Leader	Manager
Visionary	Rational
Passionate	Business-like
Creative	Persistent
Inspiring	Tough-minded
Innovative	Analytical
Courageous	Structured
Imaginative	Deliberate
Experimental	Authoritative
Independent	Stabilising
Share knowledge	Centralises knowledge
Trusting	Guarding
Warm and radiant	Cool and reserved
Expresses humility	Rarely admits to being wrong
Initiator	Implementor
Acts as coach, consultant, teacher	Acts as a boss
Does the right things	Does things right

Leadership Development	Management Development
Vision, values, clarity of mission, teamwork, managing change, communication, and culture	Financial acumen, project strategy, organising skills, process improvement, financial control, and information technology
"When it ain't broke may be the only time you can fix it"	*"If it ain't broke, don't fix it"*

Furthermore, JP Kotter in his 2001 Harvard Business Review article titled, *"What Leaders Really Do"*, depicted the differences between leaders and managers as follows:

Leadership	Management
Copes with Change	Copes with Complexity
First step is to set a direction – developing a vision for the future and strategies to achieve it	First step is to undertake planning and budgeting – setting targets or goals and steps to get there

Achieves the plan by aligning people and communicating the new direction to coalitions and teams who are committed to making it happen	Achieves the plan by organising and staffing – organisational structure, jobs, staffing the jobs, communicating the plan to staff, delegating, devising systems to monitor implementation
Achieving a vision requires motivating and inspiring and keeping the people moving in the right direction	Pursues the plan accomplishment by controlling and problem-solving and monitoring results via meetings, reports etc

So, you can see the trend emerging here from both these authors and Drucker expresses it well in the quote below.

"Management is doing things right; leadership is doing the right things."

(Peter F Drucker)

Chapter 4 Summary
What is Leadership?

How is Leadership Defined?

Leadership has been defined in numerous ways and sometimes it depends on who you might talk to. A number of definitions are given that depict how leadership is perceived. However, the over-riding theme is that leadership is about growing others, developing others, boosting others, and empowering others.

Leadership Fails

What gets in the way of real leadership? In short, autocrats or dictators and those whose egos are all about them while on the other hand, it is those leaders who abdicate responsibility and are laissez-faire as well as those being time poor, control freaks, indecisive, lack detail and who are impulsive.

Leadership that Transforms Followers

Ultimately, it's about developing followers into leaders. This is a conscious goal; the leader has a development plan in her or his head about each follower or has worked out a developmental plan in conjunction with the team member.

Leadership is about Relationships

Leaders must master the dynamics of relationships because leadership is an influence process.

Positive Leadership

This model by Prof Kim Cameron outlines the four main components to positive leadership including (1) Positive Climate (2) Positive Relationships (3) Positive Communication, and (4) Positive Meaning. Each of these areas are explained and the key activities associated with each area are outlined.

Leaders Vs Managers

There are differences and although you might spend most of your time managing, there may be on occasions, those times when you are actually in the leadership mode.

CHAPTER 5

Leadership is About Character

Being a Role Model

Regardless of whether you adhere to a transactional and/or transformational model of leadership or whatever model you might aspire to, it will mean nothing if you are first and foremost not a role model for others to follow.

Whoever is at the top of the team or organisation makes a big difference to their group, team or company. As the old saying goes, *"the fish rots from the head"*. If it is certainly true that poor or dysfunctional leadership permeates down through the team or organisation, then it is also true that effective, inspirational leadership also filters down and directly impacts the team.

"Example is not the main thing in influencing others. It is the only thing."

(Albert Schweitzer)

Remember as we have discussed previously, you are being observed constantly as a leader so you can't afford to slip up in your behaviour or actions. So, what are the characteristics of leaders that set apart those leaders who are considered effective?

"Do things for people not because of who they are or what they do in return, but because of who you are."

(Mother Theresa)

The Covey Characteristics of Leadership

Leadership is significant. We all know that. It's a bit like saying that we need oxygen to breath.

However, I have heard it said that up to 60-80% of the culture of any organisation is determined by the leader and/or its leadership team. Now, that's bit more than just breathing. So, what are the characteristics of effective leadership?

I'm sure that the list below is non-exhaustive, but it has certainly made sense to me in terms of the individuals that I have seen who have been authentic and inspiring leaders. There are **five major components** to leadership as outlined below.

1. Character

What is character? It's about Integrity, personal credibility and telling the truth.

In his book, *"Principle-Centered Leadership"*, Dr Stephen Covey has written about the importance of leaders following principles in their daily behaviour.

It's true to say that the most important quality people look for and admire in a leader is personal credibility. As Howard Morgan writes in his 2005 book *"The Art and Practice of Leadership Coaching"*, **credibility** is the foundation of leadership. If we don't believe in the messenger, we won't believe the message.

Professor Robert Goffee from the London Business School has written a book with a challenging title, namely, *"Why Should Anyone be led by You?"* A great question. What would your answer be? Why would they follow you? He goes onto to say that generally speaking, people have lost trust in leadership especially in the social and political arena. However, because of that lack of trust, people are yearning now for "authentic leadership".

In brief, being a person of character and being authentic is all about "Doing what you say you will do" or "DWYSYWD" for short. No matter where I go in visiting organisations across the planet, the message is the same re integrity. It comes in slightly different forms depending on whom I talk to, but it sounds like the following:

Practice what you preach
Walk the talk
Put your money where your mouth is
Actions speak louder than words
Have the courage of your convictions

So, how does character get defined? Try this for size.

- Making decisions with the organisation paramount in mind versus allowing a personal agenda to influence decisions
- Keeping commitments that are made
- Practicing self-development; constantly learning
- Being receptive to and specifically asking for, feedback from others
- Being approachable by anyone
- Treating everyone the same
- Treading the waitress and concierge with dignity as well as people of high status
- Trusting other people; assuming they have good intentions

- Working collaboratively with others, versus seeing everyone as a competitor
- Not acting in an arrogant manner towards others
- Being tenacious and not giving up because something is difficult
- Having emotional resilience; adjusting to rapidly changing environments

---

"The ultimate measure of a man is not where he stands in moments of comfort, but where he stands at times of challenge and controversy."

(Martin Luther King, Jr)

---

2. Personal Capability

This is all about whether you have direct knowledge or hands-on skills in relation to the industry or area in which you might lead.

I have certainly heard it said that a good leader can acquire certain technical information and expertise on the job, and that it's more about having people skills and emotional intelligence, but in the main, there is little doubt that having direct prior knowledge and expertise can assist credibility and job performance.

What would you consider personal capabilities might include?

The answer might be:

- **Technical knowledge**
- **Product or service knowledge** – a thorough understanding of what the organisation produces and why it is superior to competitive products or services
- **Problem analysis and problem-solving skills** – the ability to define a problem, analyse it, and come up with solid recommendations for resolving it
- **Professional skills** – the ability to write an intelligent, concise report; the ability to make a compelling presentation in front of a group; the ability to organise one's work in an efficient manner, to monitor progress, and to act without being told by someone in authority
- **Innovation** – the ability to have a fresh outlook in approaching a problem, to shake loose old methods and processes and see new possibilities. Innovation means being able to climb out of ruts and do things in a different fashion
- **Initiative** – the person who sees something falling in the cracks between one department and another and who immediately takes steps to make certain it is handled; it involves volunteering that something needs to be done and no one else is currently doing it
- **Effective use of information technology** – this person sets an example in the consistent use of email, powerful software applications, and any technology that escalates performance

3. Focus on Results

It is one thing to set the vision for the company or group, it is another to assist them to get there. Setting goals and providing the necessary support for the team to meet the targets is a key role for any leader.

What would you consider a focus on results might include? How do leaders focus on results? See the following list:

- Establishing stretch goals for their people
- Taking personal responsibility for the outcomes of the group
- Providing ongoing feedback and coaching to their people
- Setting loftier targets for the group to achieve
- Personally sponsoring an initiative or action
- Initiating new programs, projects, processes, client relationships, or technology
- Focusing on the organisation goals and ensuring that they are translated into actions by their department
- Operating with speed and intensity; accelerating the pace of the group
- Championing the cause of the customer or client
- Balancing long-term and short-term objectives

4. Interpersonal Skills

Leaders need to be able to connect with their followers – and connect well. Of course, it is also about being task-oriented, but what's the point of being so outcome oriented that you forget about your people?

What would you consider interpersonal skills or people skills might include? A leader with strong interpersonal skills would include the following:

- Communicating powerfully and prolifically
- Inspiring others to high-performance
- Building positive relationships with others
- Developing the skills and talents of subordinates
- Working in a collaborative manner with others
- Being an effective team member
- Recognising and rewarding the contributions of others
- Being open and receptive to new ideas
- Responding positively to feedback
- Effectively resolving conflicts within their own department and with other groups outside
- Influencing people upward in the organisation, in addition to peers and subordinates
- Building the self-esteem of others, giving positive indications of their ability to succeed
- Teaching others in a helpful manner

5. Leading Organisational Change

Anything that does not grow on the planet dies. And that goes for businesses as well. Leaders need to be able to provide the vision to their people, as well as the strategy about how to arrive and achieve the final result.

But we're creatures of habit and generally we don't like change, so the leader has to be able to guide the team through the change process which might of course, take months to achieve, but could take years.

What would you consider leading organisational change might include? What are the specific skills required for leading organisational change? Try the following:

- Has the ability to be a champion for change in the organisation
- Leads projects or programs, presenting them so that others support them
- Is an effective marketer for his or her work group's projects, programs or products
- Has a strategic perspective
- Knows his or her work relates to the organisation's business strategy (line of sight connection)
- Translates the organisation's vision and objectives into challenging and meaningful goals for others
- Takes the long view; can be trusted to balance short-term and long-term needs of the organisation
- Connects the outside world with internal groups
- Represents the work group to key groups outside the group or department
- Effectively resolving conflicts within their own department and with other groups outside
- Helps people understand how meeting customer's needs is central to the mission and goals of the organisation

So there you have it, the five major components of leadership according to Dr Stephen Covey and depicted in the figure below.

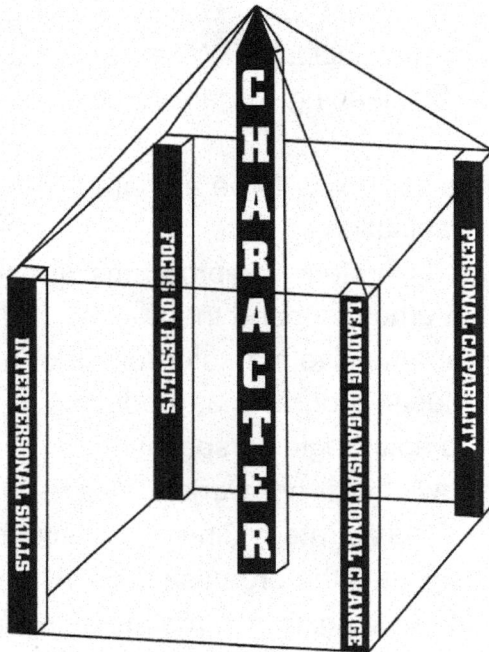

Key Leadership Skills

In an interesting article published in the McKinsey Quarterly in January 2015 by Claudio Feser and others, they reported on a comprehensive study that looked at the skills for effective leadership and they discovered a small subset of leadership skills that closely correlated with leadership success especially among frontline leaders. Not surprisingly, there is some overlap with the work of Stephen Covey, but let's look at what they found.

Using their own practical experience and searching the relevant academic literature, they came up with a comprehensive list of 20 distinct leadership traits.

They then surveyed 189,000 people in 81 diverse organisations around the globe to assess how frequently certain kinds of leadership behaviour was applied within their organisations. They then divided the sample into organisations whose leadership performance was strong and those that were weak.

What they found was that leaders in organisations with high-quality teams typically displayed **four of the 20 possible types of behavior**. These four behaviours *explained 89% of the variance or difference between strong and weak organisations* in terms of leadership effectiveness.

What were these four behaviours that differentiated effective leaders? They were as follows.

1. Being supportive

Leaders who are supportive understand and sense how other people feel. By showing authenticity and sincere interest in those around them, they build trust and inspire and help colleagues to overcome challenges. They intervene in group work to promote organisational efficiency and they allay unwarranted fears about external threats and prevent the energy of the team from dissipating with any internal conflict.

2. Operating with a strong results orientation

Leadership is about not only developing and communicating a vision and setting objectives, but also following through to achieve results. Leaders with a strong results orientation tend to emphasise the importance of efficiency and productivity and prioritise the highest value work that needs to be done.

3. Seeking different perspectives

This particular skill or trait is obvious in managers who monitor trends affecting organisations and who grasp changes occurring in the environment. In turn, they encourage employees or team members to contribute ideas that could improve performance and they also accurately differentiate between important and un-important issues as well as give appropriate weight to stakeholder concerns. Leaders who do well on this dimension typically base their decisions on sound analysis and avoid the many biases to which some decisions are prone.

4. Solving problems effectively

The process that precedes decision making is problem-solving when information is discovered, gathered, analysed and considered. This can be difficult to get right, yet it is a key input into decision-making for major issues as well as daily ones such as how to handle a team dispute.

Leadership is all about character and the work of Dr Stephen Covey as well as research from various areas highlights the kinds of factors and skills that differentiate the really effective leaders from those that don't make the grade. Information worth knowing about wouldn't you say?

"It is absurd that a man should rule others, who cannot rule himself."

(Latin Proverb)

Teamwork

One of the factors that leaders often ask about and that is critical to know, is what makes for effective teamwork. This is vital given that the Harvard Business Review in 2016 found that more that 75% of an employee's day was spent communicating with colleagues and this is often in a group or team setting.

Generally speaking, it is a given that profitability in a company increases when workers collaborate and work together. Google became focused on this issue. Google with its big data looked at all aspects of a team, but could not discern what factors were critical to team success. So, in 2012, they began "Project Aristotle" to study hundreds of their teams to find out why some teams stumbled while others soared. Input from Carnegie Mellon, M.I.T. and Union College in the USA helped determine that what distinguished "good" teams from dysfunctional ones was how teammates treated each other.

In particular, there were **two prime behaviours** that good teams shared. First, members spoke in roughly the same proportion or about the same amount. As long as *everyone got a chance to speak, the team did well*. Second, the good teams had *high social intelligence where they were skilled at intuitively knowing how others felt* on the team based on their tone, expressions and non-verbal cues. So, it was about conversational turn-taking along with empathy.

In summary, associated research by Harvard Business School professor Amy Edmondson reports that good teams therefore experienced what was termed *"psychological safety"* which is a sense of confidence that the team will not embarrass, reject or punish someone for speaking up. In other words, the team climate was one of interpersonal trust and mutual respect in which people were comfortable in being themselves.

How do leaders create this psychological safety? In one team focusing on their dynamics, the leader asked everyone to share something personal about themselves and the leader decided to go first. This opened the group up as they disclosed aspects of themselves not known to the others in the group. The group became cohesive and trusting. They all agreed to try harder to notice when someone in the group was feeling excluded or down. In other teams, they all agreed to listen to one another and show sensitivity to feelings and needs.

Vulnerabilty

One last hint. What makes someone a strong leader? One characteristic that is often overlooked is vulnerability. This sounds like a paradox, but it's true. Being vulnerable is the mark of a genuine and authentic leader. You're showing that you're human too.

The best managers acknowledge their weaknesses and aren't afraid to show their vulnerabilities. It's tempting to want colleagues and your direct reports to see you only at your best, but that's a poor way to lead. For one thing, it's not sustainable. We're all human, and we all make mistakes. Sooner or later, you will, too. For another, leading is about connecting. People will follow you, work hard for you, and sacrifice for you if they feel connected to you. And they won't feel that way if you only let them see what you think will impress them.

So don't be afraid to own up to the areas where you aren't perfect. Be prepared to acknowledge your weaknesses, your slip-ups, your mistakes and your failures. And own up to them as soon as they occur and not some time later when it might be more convenient. If it helps, think of it this way: You aren't weak; you have weaknesses. There is a difference.

"Vulnerability sounds like truth and feels like courage. Truth and courage aren't always comfortable, but they're never weakness."

(Brene Brown)

Chapter 5 Summary
Leadership is About Character

Being a Role Model
First and foremost you need to be a role model for others to follow. Setting the example is key.

The Covey Characteristics of Leadership
1. Character
2. Personal Capability
3. Focus on Results
4. Interpersonal Skills
5. Leading Organisational Change

Key Leadership Skills
A significant research study found the following aspects were critical to being an effective leader:
1. Being supportive
2. Operating with a strong results orientation
3. Seeking different perspectives
4. Solving problems effectively

Team-work
In 2012, Google began "Project Aristotle" to study hundreds of their teams to find out why some teams stumbled while others soared. In particular, there were **two prime behaviours** that good teams shared. In brief, it was about "psychological safety" where individuals in the team all got a chance to speak and the team demonstrated empathy towards each other.

Vulnerability
One characteristic that is often overlooked is vulnerability. This sounds like a paradox, but it's true. Being vulnerable is the mark of a genuine and authentic leader. You're showing that you're human too.

Leadership is all about character and the work of Dr Stephen Covey as well as research from various areas highlights the kinds of factors and skills that differentiate the really effective leaders from those that don't make the grade.

CHAPTER 6

Leadership is About Self-awareness

The Cornerstone

As the saying goes, "Self-awareness is the cornerstone of leadership". Without awareness, a leader has little (if any) hope of being an effective leader. So, how do you get to be self-aware?

The key questions here for you as a new leader include:

- Who am I really?
- How do I know myself?
- What are my values?
- What do I stand for?
- What is my mission statement?
- What are my strengths?

- How do I play to my strengths?
- How do others see me?

---

*"Strong people have a strong sense
of self-worth and self-awareness; they
don't need the approval of others."*

(Roy T Bennett)

Know Thyself

What areas would it be good to know about yourself?   What aspects would you feel comfortable talking to others about?

1. Personality

How would you describe your general personality? How would others describe you? What do family and friends say about you? What do colleagues or work peers say about you?

There are a variety of personality tests which are generally used by individuals to discover exactly who they are and what makes them 'tick'.

One such personality test which is frequently used, for instance, is the Myers-Briggs Personality Type Indicator (MBTI). The client who undergoes this test has to make a choice between two behaviour options. At the end of this process a score is presented based on four sets of scales: Introvert Vs Extravert; Intuitive Vs Sensate; Thinker Vs Feeler and Judger Vs Perceiver. The focus, for example, of being declared to be an 'ESFJ' or an 'ENFP', would be on where your energy is directed; how you process information and make decisions, and how you plan your life.

My students in the MBA course that I taught, told me about a free site for the MBTI. You might like to complete it and see how your personality style presents:

http://www.humanmetrics.com/cgi-win/jtypes1.htm

An understanding of these elements would be a most useful aid in getting to grips with the type of person you are and, by extension, with the kind of leader you might be and how you might connect with others with a different personality style.

"Your visions will become clear only when you can look into your own heart. Who looks outside dreams; who looks inside, awakes."

(Carl Jung)

2. Values

What are your values? What is important to you? What would you do if you were really wealthy and didn't have to worry about money? What do you stand for? What won't you stand for? What would you risk your life for?

In other words, what you value as a person and what you place importance on are critical to your satisfaction at work. If, for example, you place a high value on "Honesty", yet you see the company or management acting in ways that are contrary to this value, then you may feel that such a discrepancy in values leaves you with no other option than to either intervene in some way or to leave.

What are values? They are considered to be a person's principles or standards of behaviour. They constitute a judgment about what's important in life. They encapsulate our perspective on what life's priorities are all about.

Can you see how important it might be really to identify what your life values might be?

Values are those things that really matter to each of us; the notions and beliefs we hold as special. Caring for others, for example, is a value; so is financial security or quality of life. Being taken seriously or being respected is very important to some people. So is feeling that we have made a difference to others, or have left a mark on their lives in some way or contributed to their life.

What are yours? Can you clearly define them and point them out?

Most of us learned or acquired our values from our parents at home, or from our grandparents or from those who raised us. We learned our values at church or in the synagogue or temple, and at school. We formed them as we grew up and sometimes, we might change or alter our values as we grow older or more mature. A close relationship with a spouse or partner, for example, or a close relationship with one's children, is not something that one would expect an adolescent to have as a priority!

In order to have a real sense about who you are and to be confident in whom you are, you need to define your set of values. Perhaps you know them already, but just haven't taken the time to delineate them clearly. Perhaps you've kind of known what they are, but have never taken time out to write them down. Perhaps you've just somehow taken it for granted that they're there, but you're not sure how that happened or what they are exactly.

I personally see values as lighthouses for our journey in life. They act as beacons and help us to chart our journey. Of course, this doesn't mean that sometimes we might not make bad decisions or behave poorly, and when we do, we often get 'shipwrecked' and end up on the rocks, as it were. So, values are there to guide us and to protect us and assist us on our life journey. If you don't know where the lighthouses are and where the tricky regions are or where the reefs or the rocky outcrops are, then how are you going to negotiate life effectively?

"The world is full of people that have stopped listening to themselves or have listened only to their neighbours to learn what they ought to do, how they ought to behave, and what the values are that they should be living for."

(Joseph Campbell)

You'll often find too that companies have a set of corporate values. These are often displayed in prominent places or you will read about them in their annual reports or on their websites. Sadly though, they are often just words because the values don't translate into real action and the employees know it – "they ain't worth the paper they're written on" is the kind of comment sometimes made by staff.

However, I recently gave a workshop in Melbourne for a building company, and they had a clear set of values on their website that did represent what they stood for. The employees that I talked to knew it and one said that he had been trying to get into this company's workforce for some years because he knew what they were about. He said that they were renowned for being a good company to work for. Interestingly, one of the values for this company was "Value to Others". That says it all, doesn't it?

So, if it's good enough for companies and corporations to have their set of values, then it's certainly good enough for the rest of us.

If you're not able to define your set of values, then it is time that you set to work to craft them. What are your lighthouses? What's important to you? What do you stand for? What are your priorities in life?

Perhaps the best way to start to consider your personal values is to review a Values List and to begin to refine your own specific list.

At the rear of this book is an **Appendix 1** entitled **"Governing Values"**. Complete this exercise and work out your **top five personal values**. These are the values that you adhere to personally in your life. What have you got to lose?

Furthermore, in **Appendix 2, is a list of the 14 most common work values** that people look for in a job. Try to rank order them and decide what are the top five values that you really need in a job in order to be satisfied. What might be number one is non-negotiable, and number two is prime, and so on. When you look for a job, it is critical that your career contains these aspects in order for you to be fulfilled.

3. Talents

What are you good at? What do you receive compliments for? Where have you excelled in the past? Where have you been successful? What are some of your abilities?

It makes simple sense to go towards work that uses your talents and abilities. If you are doing what comes naturally, you are more likely to be happy at work. And when you're happy at work, you'll be happier in life.

Most people can do lots of things. What school subjects were your favourites? What are the things you like to do more than others? What brings a smile to your face? What do you always gravitate towards doing? What do people always tell you you're good at doing?

For example, are you good at dealing with people? If so, is it with individuals and one at a time or in groups (or both)? Perhaps you are good at taking instructions, serving or helping or maybe diagnosing, treating or healing. Maybe you are more comfortable with teams or organisations, either communicating effectively with a group or perhaps leading others in an exercise, or maybe even managing or supervising a project or running a business.

Perhaps instead, you are good at dealing with information, data and ideas. Maybe that might be gathering or creating it via research or compiling information; maybe it is through managing it, storing or retrieving it or perhaps through putting it to applied use.

Perhaps you are good at dealing with things. This might include skills with materials (eg., wood, metal, stone, gems), skills with objects (tools and instruments), skills with equipment, machinery or vehicles, skills with buildings (eg., construction or modelling), or skills with growing things including plants and animals.

Regardless of your talents, as a leader, you need to own these talents, but also be prepared to put in the work to up-skill the skills of your people and learn how to manage a team effectively.

4. Passion

What do you love to do? What activities give you satisfaction? What excites you about life? What is your secret ambition? What are your hobbies? These are valuable clues to your passions.

For example, I saw a young person who loved to write as well as to journal her thoughts and feelings, but she confessed that she hadn't done so for ages and that she had missed it. When she picked it up again, she felt that she had regained part of herself and she began to consider how writing might also become a larger part of her life in terms of a possible career.

Another client I recently saw found it so rewarding to go bushwalking. He was re-energised when he was out experiencing nature. He also loved camping and being away from the bustle of the city. Another person loved sailing and couldn't wait for the summer season to be on his boat pitting his skills against the weather and the elements as well as competing against other boats. A retired accountant I met recently told me that in his retirement he has taken up a pursuit that he has always wanted to pursue, namely, oil painting. He was loving it and had decided to take lessons as well.

Alternatively, what gets up your nose? What can't you stand? What aspects or features of our society really frustrate, annoy or upset you? In other words, are there any issues that you feel strongly about? For example, I recently saw a woman who felt very strongly about young children being abused. So much so that she decided to work in a not-for-profit organisation devoted to young people in need. Another person I saw felt very strongly about homelessness and decided as a first step that she would work in a volunteer capacity for an organisation that renders assistance to the homeless.

Knowing yourself is knowing what your passions might be.

5. Strengths

I have been at pains to say to all my clients, as well as to the MBA classes that I taught, that all of us need to play to our strengths. What happens when you work to your strengths? Dr Mihaly Csikszentmihalyi (pronounced "chicks-sent-me-high-ee") showed that real satisfaction occurs when we are **"in the flow"**. Some refer to it as it being **"in the zone"**. Professor Marty Seligman calls it the **"engaged life"** – being at one with the music, ie., being totally absorbed in what you're doing so that time seems to stop. Dr Ken Robinson calls it being **"in your element"**. In his book by the same name called *"The Element"*, it is defined as the meeting point between natural aptitude and personal passion. It's the place where the things we love to do and the things we are good at both come together.

"Play to your strengths"

(Gary Lockwood)

It's those times when you're so preoccupied by what you are doing that you lose track of time and you can't believe that so much time has really passed.

Typically, you're using your strengths and your talents and you're just caught up in the activity itself. It could have to do with being involved with your hobbies or interests, or even perhaps with romance and relationships. Maybe you're writing, sketching, working on your car, giving a presentation, building a website, babysitting the grandchildren – whatever it is, you're "in your element". These activities give us energy rather than drain us as our jobs often do. People become more alive because of these pursuits. There is little doubt that "being in the zone" increases happiness and satisfaction for people.

Do you know which of your strengths and talents have the effect of allowing you to be in your "zone"? When are you "in your element"? What do you need to do to experience more of being "in your element"?

So, play to your strengths. That is easy to say, but can you define them?

6. Character Strengths

More particularly, what are your natural character strengths? What are those strengths of character that you possess that make the good life possible? That is an interesting question.

According to a 1999 survey by Public Agenda, adults in the United States (and in most westernised countries, I would expect), cited "not learning values" as the most important problem facing today's youth (see Christopher Peterson & Martin E. P. Seligman, "Character Strengths and Virtues: A Handbook and Classification," Oxford University Press, 2004, Page 5).

From surveys of this kind, together with a push from the Positive Psychology movement, came the development of 24 character strengths that fell under six main areas of what were termed 'Virtues', namely,

Wisdom, Courage, Humanity, Justice, Temperance, and Transcendence (ie., meaning of life).

Without getting too technical, character strengths are the psychological ingredients that underpin the six main virtues in life. After thorough research and analysis starting in 2000 and spanning three years, (see Peterson & Seligman, "Character Strengths and Virtues"), a classification of 24 prime strengths were devised including such positive traits as bravery, kindness, fairness and hope. It's called the VIA of Character Strengths and you can do the survey yourself by going to the website listed below.

https://www.viacharacter.org/

Once you're on that page, click on the button that says "Take the Free VIA Survey".

What are your top five strengths? What do they say about you? Do they fall into certain virtue areas or are they spread across a number of areas?

7. Purpose & Destiny

What were you born to do? What is your unique mission in life? What does God want you to do? What are your unique opportunities? Where can you make a difference?

I know that these can be very difficult questions to ask and to answer. What is my purpose and why am I here? I also don't expect many of you to be able to trot out an answer to these questions immediately. However, having said that, they are important questions to ask and to answer.

The most important thing to know is that your career path and your move into leadership, should put you on a trajectory that is closer to, if not directly on, your *Right Path.*

In a nutshell, your *Right Path* has to do with your personal mission in life, and to do with the reason you are here. The closer you align yourself to that path, the less stress you are bound to encounter. Identifying your *Right Path* then becomes your top priority.

Being on the *Right Path* will lead to greater success, to career satisfaction and more effective leadership. When you are on your *Right Path*, obstacles will be fewer and easier to overcome. The battles you fight will at least be the right battles. Once you are on your *Right Path*, things will start to fall into place.

Your *Right Path* is like a roadmap that helps to point the way forward. Without a roadmap in life, you will be like a ship without a rudder. You will be blown this way and that. The slightest breeze will knock you off course.

So, how do you go about seeking to examine and to answer this question in relation to your purpose or destiny? What is your mission statement? Yes, I know that companies and corporates have them, but if it's okay for them, then it's certainly okay for each of us.

"A man without a purpose is like a ship without a rudder — a waif, a nothing, a no man"

(Thomas Carlyle)

I really like the exercise that Dr Stephen Covey has to offer as a way of allowing us to get more in touch with our destiny and our purpose (Stephen R Covey, "The 7 Habits of Highly Effective People," The Business Library, 1989, Page 96-97).

He suggests finding a place where you can be alone and uninterrupted. Have a pen and paper with you because you'll be doing some writing. Relax, clear your mind of "stuff" and be open to the experience.

Now, in your mind's eye, see yourself going to a funeral of a loved one. Picture yourself driving to the funeral parlour or chapel, parking the car, and getting out. As you walk inside the building, you notice the flowers and the soft organ music. You see the faces of friends and family as you pass along the way. You feel the shared sorrow of losing, the joy having known, that radiates from the hearts of the people gathered there. As you walk down to the front of the room and look inside the casket to pay your last respects, you suddenly come face to face with yourself. This is **your** funeral, three years from today. All these people have come to honour you, to express feelings of love and appreciation for your life.

As you take a seat and wait for the service to begin, you look at the program in hand. There are four speakers. The first is from your family, immediate and also extended – children, brothers, sisters, nephews, nieces, aunts, uncles, cousins, and grandparents who have come from all over to attend. The second speaker is one of your friends, someone who can give a sense of who you are as a person. The third speaker is from your work or profession. And the fourth is from your church, sport or community organisation where you've been involved in service.

Now think deeply. What would you like each of these speakers to say about you and your life? What kind of husband, wife, father, mother, would you like their words to reflect? What kind of son, daughter or cousin? What kind of friend? What kind of working associate, peer or colleague?

What character would you like them to have seen in you? What contributions, what achievements would you want them to remember? Look carefully at the people around you? What difference would you like to have made in their lives?

In **Appendix 3**, take a few minutes to jot down your impressions. After you've done that exercise, now consider **your own eulogy.** What do you want your eulogy to consist of? What would matter most at the end of your life? What do you want to be remembered for? Write it out in full. Be proud of it. Own it.

This is your destiny, this is your purpose.

Without a vision of where you are supposed to go, your life will seem like a bunch of random events. Let it not be a wasted life. Choose how you'd like to be remembered and then live life according to that script. This life is not a dress rehearsal; this is it, so live it fully and to your best.

Feedback is the Breakfast of Champions

As Tony Robbins says repeatedly, "Feedback is the breakfast of champions". How do we know ourselves? Typically, through how others might see us.

Naturally, asking for feedback from those around us can be a daunting exercise for some and certainly for most, it creates some sort of anxiety. A leader therefore that refuses to seek feedback and understand how they are being perceived probably shouldn't be a leader at all. This kind of behaviour which is resistant to any kind of feedback is probably indicative of someone who is either very insecure or else, indicative of a huge ego who knows it all and who can't be told anything. Either way, it is hardly a recommendation for leadership.

Of course, how others see us might not always be accurate, but if there is a consensus across various people, it may well be more accurate than you think.

An effective exercise to ascertain whether how you see yourself is comparable to how others see us is by using the Johari Window Exercise. **Appendix 4** outlines that particular exercise. In this case, it's probably best to find a colleague or work peer (either from your current or previous workplace) who you can trust and who is happy to give you feedback and engage in this exercise.

What is Your Leadership Style?

To help you further become aware, it might be helpful to complete the Leadership Diagnostic:

https://leadershipcoaching.com.au/leadership-diagnostic/

Although this is a self-report instrument, it ought to give you an idea about your specific strengths as a leader and then help you focus on those aspects that are lacking or ineffective in order to shore up your overall abilities.

Chapter 6 Summary
Leadership is About Self-awareness

The Cornerstone
As the saying goes, "Self-awareness is the cornerstone of leadership". Without awareness, a leader has little (if any) hope of being an effective leader.

Know Thyself
What areas would it be good to know about yourself and therefore feel comfortable talking to others about such aspects? Tips are given about how you can explore each of the areas below:
1. Personality
2. Values
3. Talents
4. Passion
5. Strengths
6. Character Strengths
7. Purpose & Destiny

Feedback is the Breakfast of Champions
How do we know ourselves? Typically, through how others might see us. Of course, how others see us might not always be accurate, but if there is a consensus across various people, it may well be more accurate than you think. Do you have the courage to ask for feedback?

What is Your Leadership Style?
Complete the Leadership Diagnostic to give you more information about your strengths.

CHAPTER 7

Leadership is About Emotional Intelligence

The Foundation Stone

This topic has captured the imagination of the business world especially over the last couple of decades or so where we are now studying what it takes for people to be able to step up and for a leader to be able to really lead.

So what is Emotional Intelligence (EI)? In a nutshell, it's about being aware of our thoughts and feelings, managing these, and therefore being able to connect more effectively with those around us. It's about how we manage our personality if you like.

Interestingly, research shows that our mental intelligence (ie., IQ) predicts no more than 25% of our performance (JE Hunter, "Validity and utility of alternate predictors of job performance," Psychological Bulletin, 96, 72-98). So, what predicts the other 75%? In the mid 1990s, Daniel Goleman popularized the notion of Emotional Intelligence and indicated that this was the main factor contributing to job performance. *"We are being judged by a new yard stick; not just how smart we are, or by our training and expertise, but also how well we handle ourselves and each other"* ("Working with EI", 1998*)*.

Further, Goleman ("What Makes a Leader," Harvard Business Review, Nov-Dec. 1998) went on to say that:

"When I compared leaders who were linked to strong performance with average performers, 90% of the difference was attributable to emotional intelligence rather than technical skills". My entire education over-developed my IQ skills and nowhere along the line did anyone ever teach me social skills, interpersonal skills – more importantly, emotional skills – which are at the centre of developing trust."

In fact, Goleman went so far as to state that, *"EI is twice as important as any other factor in predicting outstanding employee performance."*

In Summary, what does this all mean?
- In recent years, many different aspects of emotions, motives, and personality that help determine interpersonal effectiveness and

leadership skill have been placed under one comprehensive label of **Emotional Intelligence**.

- These factors are related to success in life
- Helps us understand why some people do well in life and others struggle or fail
- Distinct from IQ (cognitive intelligence)
- Distinct from our personality which is relatively fixed (probably since birth)
- EI can be developed and changed

The evidence for the effectiveness of EI in the business arena in particular, has been steadily mounting, but there have been those who have purported otherwise:

- **EI is something you are born with**
  As hinted at above, EI is based on attitudes and habits, neither of which you are born with. The big benefit therefore is that EI can be developed by anyone.
- **EI is just a fad**
  It certainly was popularized in the 1990s, but it has been used widely in education and business since the 1980s and different terms have been around for similar concepts since 1920.
- **EI is really just naval gazing**
  Developing EI certainly demands self-awareness, but it goes beyond that to doing something about your thoughts and feelings and taking action that is observable to others.

- **EI is just soft stuff**

  As is the way with many things, the soft stuff is really the hard stuff. Having an open and honest conversation with someone, delegating work that is not popular, disagreeing with someone, resolving conflict are all hard for most of us.

- **EI is just soft skills**

  EI is much more than soft skills. Skills such as assertiveness can support EI, but need to be backed up by deeper attitudes and changes in behaviour.

- **Women are more emotionally intelligent**

  There is evidence that females are better than males at empathy and relationship skills for example, while for some other factors (eg., achieving and reaching goals) males tend to do better.

- **EI is simply about being nice to others**

  EI is definitely about having regard for others, but this does not mean that you have to like their behaviour. The difficult part is still valuing a person despite maybe disapproving of their behaviour.

Goleman's Model of Emotional Intelligence

Goleman put forward the notion that there were **four main aspects** to emotional intelligence as follows.

1. Self-awareness

This involves being self-aware and having self-confidence (knowing what one feels) and being able to recognise feelings appropriately, as they happen; and understanding how feelings affect performance; accurate self-awareness (as has been mooted above) is the core competency of emotional intelligence.

2. Social Awareness

This is about being able to recognise other's emotions, be interested in them, understand their situation and how they feel in such circumstances as well as accurately and sensitively communicate that to others. It is about understanding the emotional currents, politics, and climate as well as power relationships within organisations. In essence, it is about accurately reading the politics and understanding what is appropriately and realistically possible given the circumstances. It is about being aware of service responsibilities, and in particular recognising and striving to meet stakeholder and customer needs.

3. Self-management

This is about effectively controlling one's emotions such as anger and anxiety especially when they could get out of hand and be inappropriate. This also includes being adaptable which includes being flexible in solving problems and managing change based on reality and facts.

4. Social Skills

This really is about how individuals who are emotionally competent actually relate and connect with others. This includes the ability to influence and lead others for example, by guiding, and directing individuals and groups toward a goal. Sometimes this might be related to inspiring, energising, or directing change and at times resolving conflict. It also includes assessing the developmental needs of others and perhaps teaching, instructing or coaching them to develop particular skills and competencies. It also includes the use of positive feedback, praise and reinforcement. This aspect of emotional intelligence is about working collaboratively and cooperatively with individuals and teams in order to achieve specific goals.

In short, solid research supports the notion that emotional self-awareness is a prime pre-requisite for self-management which in turn predicts social skills, particularly empathy, which in turn governs one's ability to manage relationships effectively.

Bar-On Emotional Competency Model

This whole notion of emotional intelligence was picked up by a psychological test publisher called Bar-On and among other things, they developed a more comprehensive model of what it means to be successful with strong emotional intelligence. Their recipe for success was according to the following table:

Self-Awareness	Social Awareness
All 3 Competencies	**Empathy Plus 1 of:**
• Emotional Self-Awareness • Accurate Self-Assessment • Self-Confidence	• Organisational Awareness • Service Orientation
Self-Management	**Relationship Management**
Emotional Self-Control Plus 1 of:	**Influence Plus 1 of:**
• Transparency • Adaptability	• Developing Others • Inspirational Leadership • Change Catalyst
OR	**OR**
• Achievement Orientation • Initiative • Optimism	• Conflict Management • Teamwork & Collaboration

In case you need to understand what some of these terms might mean, please see below.

Self-Awareness

- Emotional Self-Awareness = recognising our emotions and their effects
- Accurate Self-Assessment = knowing our strengths and limits
- Self-Confidence = a strong sense or our self-worth and capabilities

Self-Management

- Self-Control = keeping disruptive emotions and impulses under control
- Transparency = maintaining honesty & integrity
- Adaptability = flexibility in adapting to changing situations or obstacles
- Achievement Orientation = the guiding drive to meet internal standards of excellence
- Initiative = readiness to act
- Optimism = a positive attitude

Social Awareness

- Empathy = understanding others and taking an active interest in their concerns
- Organisational Awareness = understanding and empathising (issues, dynamics, politics) at the organisational level
- Service Orientation = recognising and servicing customer needs

Relationship Management
- Developing Others = sensing others' developmental needs and bolstering their abilities
- Inspirational Leadership = inspiring and guiding groups of people
- Change Catalyst = initiating or managing change
- Conflict Management = resolving disagreements
- Teamwork & Collaboration = working with others towards shared goals

Now what this means is that you don't have to be an expert in all areas in relation to emotional intelligence. However, the Bar-On framework suggests a recipe for success that involves each of the four major areas as listed above, but recognising that there are key components to each of these areas which would be folly to overlook as a leader.

"If you want to be something different – you have to do something different"

(Author unknown)

Case Studies

James came to see me because he worked in a government department, but had now been passed over twice for a promotion. He said he was confused because he put his head down and worked hard. He didn't take breaks like others might or hang around the photocopier or the watercooler and chat. He got on with his work. He said that he didn't like to bother his boss and only ever talked to his boss if there was a major problem with his work that he couldn't fix. He was somewhat shy and didn't attend any of the functions that the social club organised.

We discussed the importance of EI. James agreed to try some different things since what he had been doing to date certainly hadn't been working. He had various "homework" tasks to do including, saying hello to people each day, letting his boss know at least once a week what he was working on, visiting the watercooler and making conversation and attending at least one social function over a three month period.

James reported that he was feeling much happier at work, and that people were more friendly towards him. He hadn't had a chance to apply for any jobs, but he was feeling more confident about the prospect.

Frank on the other hand, had been recommended to receive coaching by the HR Manager based in Sydney. Frank was a State Manager (in another State) who had a reputation for "not suffering fools gladly". The turn-over in his senior management team was high and he was unsure why this might be so. We instituted a 360 degree feedback for Frank so that he could receive information regarding his personal performance from those above him, his peers, and his direct reports. The results showed his inability to listen and empathise, his poor communication skills and his inability to develop team relationships. Frank was initially offended at the results suggesting that they were all "out to get him", but later agreed to see if he could change his behaviour. We will institute another 360 survey in about 12 month's time to see how he has progressed.

Chapter 7 Summary
Leadership is About Emotional Intelligence

The Foundation Stone
Goleman (who popularised the notion of EI in the 1990s) went so far as to state that, *"EI is twice as important as any other factor in predicting outstanding employee performance."*

Goleman's Model of Emotional Intelligence
The model depended on four main aspects:
1. Self-awareness
2. Social Awareness
3. Self-management
4. Social Skills

Bar-On Emotional Competency Model
This model goes further than the Goleman model and gives more detail about what aspects of EI really count.

Case Studies
How EI plays out in the workplace.

CHAPTER 8

Leadership is About Understanding Human Behaviour

The Six Basic Needs

Why do we do what we do? As leaders, it is important to understand what makes us "tick" and have a sense about what motivates and drives your team.

Much of your happiness lies in satisfying your basic needs. You have six, in case you didn't know. Let me tell you about your six basic needs, and let me reiterate that they need to be satisfied in order for you (and your team) to find some happiness and success in life. I first heard this framework put forward at a workshop conducted by Tony Robbins and since then, have found that it really does help to explain so many aspects of why people behave the way that they do.

"Men take only their needs into consideration -- never their abilities."

(Napoleon Bonaparte)

In relation to these needs, there is a qualifier too. Each of these needs can be satisfied either in a positive way or in a negative way, so, of course, we want to approach them in a positive way. The first four needs are for survival; the last two needs are for fulfillment.

1. Security, Control and Sameness

The first need is **security and sameness or certainty and control**. You need to have some routine and control in your life. You need things to be fairly consistent, and maintain a sense of sameness. You need certainty and security. We like things to stay the same in order to avoid stress and to gain pleasure in life. In a sense, it's survival. We like to be certain about things and to be in control.

Think about a time when you were uncertain, when you felt insecure. Perhaps you were uncertain about your health, your finances or your children. It's likely that you were also unhappy at that time. So it's true we need security, we need sameness and control in order to feel more content.

To satisfy this need in a positive way, it is helpful to keep a diary or schedule, and to manage your time effectively. To satisfy this need in a negative way is to be a "control freak" (and we probably all know someone who fits this label) or to be obsessive or compulsive. Managers and supervisors who are high on this need are micro-managers (and don't we hate this kind of style).

2. Variety

We also need **variety,** and we need different kinds of experiences in our lives. It's the flip-side of the first need. It's the other side of the coin, isn't it? Variety is the spice of life! In a sense, we need some uncertainty (as strange as that may seem). If you have too much sameness or certainty all the time, you are going to be very bored. In fact, **it has been said that the quality of your life is dependent upon how much variety or uncertainty you have in your life**. It's the juice of life.

To satisfy this need positively, we vary our lives. We take a vacation in a different place each year, go to different restaurants, travel to work by different routes, try different foods, meet new people, join a new group, try a new hobby and so on.

Satisfying this need negatively, for example, is to binge on alcohol, take illicit drugs, gamble, have "one night stands," and so on.

3. Significance and Importance

The third aspect we need is to have **significance and importance** in our lives. There are a number of ways that we get a sense of significance and importance. It might be by achieving (eg., gaining qualifications, getting a promotion, forging a career, losing weight, getting fitter), or getting material possessions (eg., buying your first home, getting that car, saving for that overseas holiday).

In a negative way, people gain a sense of importance by tearing others down and being abusive, or on the other hand, they get noticed by playing "sick", and being the "victim". They can also pursue this need negatively by living for goods and material possessions, having only designer-label clothes, driving only the latest BMW or Lexus, bragging about their latest trip to Europe or some other exotic place. Their identity is wrapped up in the superfluous trappings of material goods.

Interestingly, though, the more that people become important and significant (eg., going up the corporate ladder and gaining responsibility and power), the more isolated they tend to become and separate, and that brings us to the fourth need (which is the flip-side of the third need).

4. Love and Connection

We need to have **love and connection to someone else (eg., your spouse, a friend) or perhaps something else (eg., nature, your garden, a pet)**. It's all about relationships, connecting to others, bonding and communicating. Whether we like it or not, we are a gregarious people. We were built to interact and socialise.

This need therefore might be met through caring for or providing a service to someone else, being part of a friendship, or having a romantic relationship. For some people it might mean having and caring for a pet.

On the negative side, we might satisfy this need through gaining sympathy through sickness or injury, and playing "poor me".

As I hinted at above, because the need for connection is so strong, the leader or manager (or politician?) who becomes more important and significant in life usually lets work get in the way of his or her family responsibilities and therefore becomes dis-connected from the spouse and children. Because he or she still needs love and connection, they get "re-connected" by having an affair and usually to someone in their office or workplace.

This notion of being connected to others though is consistent with the research finding from Professor Seligman and his associates that relationships with those around us are paramount to happiness. Whether it be with family or friends, connection with others is important to one's happiness and success. The research is very clear on this.

In fact, there is an amazing longitudinal study across 75 years conducted by Dr Robert Waldinger (Clinical Professor of Psychiatry at Harvard Medical School and Director of the Harvard Study of Adult Development). He (and others before him) examined what factors contributed to a good life and a satisfying life. Was it wealth, status, fame, power or position?

Firstly, it was discovered that **healthy connections** are positive for us as individuals. In contrast, loneliness creates a toxic environment where people are less happy, health declines earlier in mid-life, brain functioning deteriorates earlier and these people also live shorter lives. Within the USA at least, 1 in 5 persons report being lonely. What does that do for the health of a nation?

Secondly, it is not just about having friends or being in a committed relationship, it is about **the quality of those close relationships**. Living in a connected warm relationship is both positive and is protective. On the other hand, living in the midst of conflict such as in a poor marriage, is bad for our health and is actually worse than getting divorced.

Interestingly, at age 50 years, the greatest predictor of health and satisfaction was those who were engaged in a positive relationship. *Those most healthy in their 80s, were those most satisfied in their relationship in their 50s.*

Thirdly, the research found that good, positive relationships not only protect our bodies, but also **protect our brains**. In other words, having secure and attached relationships where you can count on another person in times of need, when the going got tough, the other was there to support and care, meant that our brain functioning in our 80s was significantly healthier. Those individuals who were in poor relationships had earlier memory decline. Ponder on that for a moment.

So, what's the message?

In an age where we want a quick fix to a happy and satisfying life and where there is the myth that it's all about wealth and riches, fame and fortune, nothing is further from the truth.

Instead, **a satisfying and healthy life is about positive relationships with family, friends and community.**

"The grand essentials of happiness are: something to do, something to love, and something to hope for."

(Allan K. Chalmers)

Satisfying these four needs therefore, will give you a sense of happiness if they are met in positive ways.

However, *there are two more needs, and meeting these needs can provide fulfillment* (not just satisfaction).

5. Personal Growth

Personal growth and development is the fifth need. Life is about growth and learning. Anything on the planet that doesn't grow, dies.

It's about extending yourself, developing yourself, learning new things, and stepping out. It could involve reading, listening to a download on your mp3 player or smart phone or watching a movie on your i-pad. Maybe it's about learning a new skill such as public speaking or wood turning. Maybe it involves attending a vocational educational course or a set of lectures. My mother-in-law, for instance, was is in her 80s, when she attended a history course at the Third Age University for seniors, which she thoroughly enjoyed. My own parents when they were in their late 80's decided to finally learn to use a computer and attend various courses for seniors.

Fulfilling this need means trying new things, going to new places, and meeting new people – whatever it takes for you to extend yourself to learn and grow.

6. Leaving a Legacy

The final basic need which provides fulfillment is **leaving a legacy and making a contribution**. This is going beyond yourself; making a contribution to society and giving of yourself. That might mean that you join, volunteer for, or assist with a charity or community group. Perhaps it means giving money or assisting with fund-raising; giving of your time and/or knowledge; passing on skills or information. Maybe it means being a mentor to someone younger than yourself perhaps in your company or in the general community.

This is also parallel to Professor Martin Seligman's framework for happiness and satisfaction being associated with living a meaningful life (see his book titled *"Flourish"* published in 2011).

In summary, in order to attain happiness and fulfillment, we need to make sure that we have satisfied all of these needs in our lives and in positive ways. We need to find ways in which to satisfy them, not only within ourselves, but in our family, in our work, and in our communities.

If we don't satisfy these six basic needs, we are lopsided. People who are lopsided are stressed and, needless to say, not happy or fulfilled.

Implications for Leadership

Now think about these six basic needs in relation to leadership. If you think about those bosses who have been difficult to work for and who have caused you the most grief, chances are that they have majored in satisfying Need 1 (Control) and Need 3 (Significance & Importance). Without doubt, these bosses cause the most heartache in the workplace creating a toxic culture including bullying and harassment as well as having favourites and forming clichés and are the primary cause of people leaving their jobs.

On the other hand, think of those leaders in the world who have made a substantial positive impact. For example, consider people like Nelson Mandella, Martin Luther King, Jr., and Mother Theresa. What needs would you say that they majored in? You guessed it. Need 6 (Contribution), Need 5 (Personal Growth) and Need 4 (Love and Connection). Perhaps you've been fortunate enough to have worked with leaders like this.

What do we learn from this?

The happiest bosses or leaders to work for are **not** those who are promulgating themselves and their egos through needs 1 and 3, but instead are concentrating on needs 4-6. Interestingly, and here's another paradox – those leaders who uphold needs 4-6 as a way of living, also receive needs 1-3 as a bonus! Now isn't that something to think about!

Chapter 8 Summary
Leadership is About Understanding Human Behaviour

It is important to understand how we "tick". In short, we have 6 basic needs that have to be satisfied in a positive way in order for us to not only survive, but to be fulfilled. Each of these needs can be played out within ourselves privately, within our family, at work or in the community.

Sadly though, the reason for our dissatisfaction in life is often that we either don't satisfy our basic needs or we satisfy them in negative or sabotaging ways.

These basic needs which explain all our behaviour and point the way to happiness include the following:
1. Control / Security / Certainty
2. Variety / Uncertainty
3. Significance / Importance
4. Love / Connection
5. Personal Growth / Development
6. Leaving a Legacy / Making a Contribution

Implications for Leadership
In relation to leadership, not only do these needs help us understand our team and why they might do what they do, but the best bosses are those who put certain needs above others such as needs 4-6.

CHAPTER 9

Communication

There is no doubt at all that the one skill that outstanding leaders have in spades is the ability to communicate effectively not only in getting their message across, but more particularly in being able to listen and understand the message being given to them. **Of all the skills that you as a new leader need to become exceptional at, it's the ability to communicate well and especially listen.**

In fact, this particular skill is so critical to your role as the new leader and so critical in relation to your overall career progression that I devoted a book to the subject titled, *"Listen Up Now: How to increase growth and profit by really listening to your customers and clients".* I mentioned this in an earlier chapter. I would encourage you to gain a hard copy of the book through www.Amazon.com (or www.Amazon.com.au if you're in Australia) or else download an audio copy so that you can listen for example while driving in the car or at other times (go to www.ListenUpnow.com.au).

I don't wish to repeat the contents of that book here except to point out some critical aspects of this notion in relation to communication. In my opinion, standout leaders are outstanding at both listening and asking key questions. Mastering these two skills ought to be at the top of your development list.

We all have ears to hear and are not deaf and yet we often have difficulty trying to understand the message that others are trying to express. Why so? Listening is not the same thing as hearing. The latter is a passive act which does not require you to really participate. Instead, listening is an active act which demands attention. As you well know, if you stop to think about it, you can hear every word of the statement, and yet have not paid an atom of attention to it. You heard with your ears, but you did not listen.

"Most people do not listen with the intent to understand; they listen with the intent to reply."

(Stephen R Covey)

The Five Levels of Listening

There are various levels of listening. It is important to recognise that there is just not one level. There are actually five. Let's name them.

1. Ignoring. This really doesn't need any explanation. It's fairly self-evident. You don't pay attention at all. You're dis-engaged.

2. Pretending. This is recognised by responses like "yeah", "uh-huh", "right".

3. Selective Listening. This is recognised by the person who only hears certain parts of the conversation. Most of us are guilty at times of doing this.

4. Active Listening. This is when the person pays attention to the words being said.

5. Empathic Listening. This is listening with intent to really understand what is being said and to really understand the feelings being expressed.

What is Listening?

Do you know what it actually is? Could you describe to a work colleague or family friend what it actually entails or what is required? Could you accurately describe the skills inherent in listening?

1. Empathy: listening is being able to show empathy for a person, which means experiencing with the other what they feel and think.   This means entering actively and imaginatively into the other person's situation and trying to understand a frame of reference and a perspective different from your own.

It means not only hearing the words, but picking up the feeling tones, even perhaps the meaning that might be somewhat hidden for the speaker. Can we sense the shape of the other person's inner world? Can we put ourselves in their shoes and appreciate what it is like to be them?

In the novel, *"To Kill a Mockingbird"*, listening appropriately to another person is described as the ability to jump inside the skin of the other person and walk around and see the world through the eyes of the other.

2. Asking questions: a good listener does not merely remain silent, but is prepared to ask questions without any hint of skepticism or challenge or hostility (whether in wording or non-verbally).

Such questions need to be clearly motivated by genuine curiosity about the speaker's view and as such could be called "questions for clarification". These questions simply request more information (eg., "Can you expand on that point?" "Can you state that argument again?" "Can you repeat that please?")

3. Giving feedback: the listener must communicate to the other that he or she has heard, and critically, this needs to be done in a non-judgmental, accepting, non-evaluative and caring way. Therefore, saying things like, "What you are really saying is..." or "Summarising what you've said..." allows the other person to know if you are 'on target' and are correct in what you consider you have heard.

4. A learned skill: it is not innate, but is an acquired skill that has to be practiced and worked at (like many other skills in life).

Being able to intensively listen to another is actually a gift to them. It is truly redemptive to others and creative.

Redemptive because when someone really hears us and sensitively understands, it frees us from the fear of ourselves and our inadequacies and feelings of lack of self-worth. It shows respect for what we think and feel. It gives a message that we count, our opinions count and our feelings count. We matter.

"If we can share our story with someone who responds with empathy and understanding, shame can't survive."

(Brene Brown)

Redemptive because we become more whole and re-own those parts of us that we have previously shut away. Creative because it unleashes new energy in us to grow, to find new goals to reach, to find new solutions to issues. It encourages us to move on and continue to be our best and manage the challenges in life.

Listening is a very real gift. It's one that is given to all of us if we wish to use it and practice it and its power is absolutely profound. **Are you using your gift?**

This might seem all a bit too "soft" for business using our "gifts" such as listening or too "soft" for leadership. As I said, our greatest handicap in life is ourselves, in that we cut off through our personal filters, things that could well be of significant benefit to us.

Leave your mind open and put your filters down and put your agendas away.

What have you got to lose? If you really give listening a go, a real go, and apply this new skill and it doesn't work, you can go back to your old way of doing things.

What It Is Not

"Listening" is **not** any one of the following:

1. Maintaining a polite silence: listening does not mean simply maintaining a polite silence while you are rehearsing in your head the speech you are going to make the next time your partner stops talking and you can grab a conversational opening.

2. Mowing others down: listening does not mean waiting alertly for flaws in the other person's arguments so that later, you can mow him or her down.

3. Having all the answers and giving advice: listening does not mean that you are supposed to come up with all the necessary answers to problems or issues or be especially knowledgeable and wise and sophisticated. Regardless, can you ever know "what is best" for the other person when they have a totally different life experience from you?

4. Giving inappropriate minimal responses: listening is not simply a case of saying "I see" or "yes" or "uh-huh" at various pauses or at specific times in the conversation when you think it seems appropriate to do so.

5. Playing "psychiatrist": listening is not trying to be insightful and interpretive and kind of "big dealing" yourself by being in touch with the latest theories on human dynamics and human development.

6. Parroting: listening is not regurgitating back to your partner word for word what you have directly heard like a recorder play-back does nor does it mean being like a "parrot".

7. Sympathy: listening is not showing sympathy **for** a person nor feeling **for** the other person.

8. Automatic skill: listening is not just something that comes naturally, where everyone is just sort of born with it and everyone has an in-built ability to be able to listen and communicate with others around them.

"The word 'listen' contains the same letters as the word 'silent'."

(Alfred Brendel)

Why Don't We Listen?

Interestingly, in my experience most people (not to mention leaders) believe that they are good listeners. I certainly remember an introductory group exercise where people had to disclose their particular strengths and talents and the woman I was paired with felt that she was a very effective listener. However, she could not remember my name nor much about what I had discussed with her when she was asked to feed it back to the group.

What is it then that prevents us from really listening to what others are saying to us? What headset are we in that means we do not take on board what others are saying? What mind-set do we have? Typically, people who are **not** good listeners often fall into the following categories:

- **Reassurer**: this is where people are quick to reassure or play down something (instead of really listening to what is being said) and say things like, "It will be okay" or "It's nothing to worry about" or "No big deal".
- **Mind reader**: this is where you might be trying to go beyond the words with such thoughts as "What is this person really thinking or feeling?" and maybe even putting thoughts or interpretations onto things which simply aren't there.
- **Filterer**: you might be tempted to call this selective listening where you only hear what you want to hear.
- **Placater**: this is where you agree with everything you hear just to be nice or to avoid conflict which probably means you're not really listening at all because you're so intent on being liked and being "nice".
- **Advice-Giver**: this is where you jump in quickly and prematurely with a fix, a solution, recommendation or advice which may in fact, be quite off the mark because you have not yet heard the full story or gotten all the details.
- **Dreamer**: this is where you might drift off during a face-to-face conversation and be consumed in your own thoughts to a point where you might

have to say in a somewhat embarrassing way, "What did you say?" or "Could you repeat that?"

- **Identifier**: this is where you might interpret everything you hear to your own experience so that you really miss what is being said, and instead, simply end up talking about yourself and your experiences.

- **Derailer**: this is where you change the subject too quickly which sends a message to the other person that you're not really interested in anything that they have to say.

- **Interrupter**: this is where you jump in on another person's conversation and cut off what they are saying which really means that you don't hear the essence of what they are talking about and also sends the message that what you have to say is far more important than their comments.

- **Rehearser**: as mooted above, this is by far the most common where you are so busy rehearsing in your head what you can say when you can grab a conversational opening that you have little idea of what the individual has actually just said.

In essence, the failure to listen is really about our own egos taking over where we find it difficult to put ourselves aside where we give time, effort and energy to the other person and where we should concentrate on what they are saying with their story, their feelings and their thoughts.

For various reasons as listed above, we get in the road with our own egos and our own agendas which stops us from being able to effectively listen.

"You have two ears and one mouth and you need to use them in that proportion."

(Author unknown)

The Art of Listening

Basically, there are **5 specific skills** that make up listening.
1. Stop and Look
2. Suspend Your Judgment
3. Paraphrase their Content
4. Acknowledge their Feelings
5. Summarise

It's true to say that these skills are absolutely critical to listening. If you don't get these right, you can forget about being a good communicator. Let's take each in turn.

1. Stop and Look

Paying attention is putting aside what you are doing, turning to face the person, and making eye contact.

The eye contact does not need to be "staring", but comfortable. Maintain eye contact and do not do something else at the same time (eg., flick over some pages, glance at the monitor or screen, watch the TV etc).

"The way that we start our conversation often determines the outcome of the communication"

Facial expression needs to be relaxed and perhaps smiling. At least you don't want to look poker-faced. It is important to non-verbally indicate that you are giving the person your time and attention. Remember, your non-verbals say a whole lot!

2. Suspend Your Judgment

Suspension of judgement is when you put your own views or your own agendas to one side. In other words, the leader or manager attempts to understand the other person's situation without imposing his or her own assumptions and values on it all. Don't be too quick to judge. Don't be too quick to evaluate.

This takes patience and respect.

The listener or manager must demonstrate an attitude of what is called "unconditional positive regard" toward the other person whether that be a client, customer or staff member. The listener makes his or her attention available independent of the other person's behaviour. This serves to assure the other person that the listener will listen without imposing conditions on their opinions or behaviour.

In actual terms, suspending judgement involves allowing time for **the other person's message to sink in** without trying to make decisions about it or jumping to conclusions about their issue or jumping in at all.

The listener who suspends judgement is likely to...
- check out his or her assumptions (*"Are you really saying that....?"*)
- request clarification from the other person (*"I'm not sure what you meant by.....?"*)
- and endeavour to understand the meanings the other person places on the particular issue or situation (*"So what you're really saying is..."*)

Suspending judgement communicates respect and acceptance to the other person.

Of course, we all have judgements and opinions about other people and what they might have said or done. However, in this "listening conversation", such opinions are put at the back of the mind and not at the front of the mind. There is a difference!

In other words, while we hold our opinions, we do not let them out, we do not say them and we "reserve judgement".

3. Paraphrasing

In **paraphrasing**, the listener or manager attempts to feed back to the client or staff member the essence of what he or she has just said, but in a restated form.

Paraphrasing often centres more on **what** the other person said than **how** they said it. Paraphrasing is useful in clarifying confusing verbal content, in tying together a number of recent comments and in highlighting issues by stating them more concisely.

Paraphrasing content achieves **four** specific purposes:

(1) It **conveys** to the other person that the listener is with the person and is trying to understand what the person is saying.
(2) It helps to **crystallize** a person's comments by repeating what he or she has said in a more concise manner, and in the listener's own words.
(3) It provides **a check** for the listener's own perceptions and verifies whether or not the listener really does understand what the other person is saying.
(4) It helps the other person **to move further** and talk more extensively on the topic.

This skill is really a first basic step.

It is relatively easy to do. It is simply giving feedback to the other person about what you think that you just heard. Having said that, although it might be the easiest, most just don't do it. Strange really.

4. Acknowledge Feelings

This skill involves being alert to and responding to the **feeling** being expressed, rather than attending solely to the **content** of what the person has said.

It is the ability to be with the person emotionally. It is therefore a very powerful skill. Not only is it important to paraphrase what you heard as we discussed above, but to also reflect back the feelings in full.

What the other person is saying is the *content* portion of the message being communicated, but one must also listen to **how** the person says what he or she does.

For example:
- the person may speak more quickly when communicating enthusiasm,
- wave their hands around when being excited,
- look down with shoulders hunched over when communicating being "down",
- move slowly when communicating discouragement and so forth.

Alternatively, the person may use specific feeling words such as 'depressed', 'down', 'anxious', 'tense', 'annoyed', 'stressed-out', 'excited' or 'happy'.

Being alert to and responding to the feeling being expressed is a skill which is appropriate at most times:

- Regardless of the nature of the feeling (whether it is positive, negative or 'in-between'), and
- Regardless of the direction of expression (towards one-self, towards others, the listener or the conversation situation).

Of all the skills, *this one of **Acknowledging their Feelings** is the hardest*. Why?

It is the most difficult because it creates "fear" amongst people simply because leaders and managers believe that they cannot control emotions and feelings and they believe that it might all "get out of control" (and that would be awful!). This is a myth because customers and staff generally won't allow themselves to get out of control anyway. Even if the other person did happen to get "out of control", then using the listening skills allows the leader to get back on track.

Furthermore, **the real reality is that if the leader or manager do tap into the emotion, the other person will feel listened to like no other skill can do**. The real question then, is **whether the leader has the courage** to use the reflection of feeling. Are you up for it?

As an aside, being a psychologist meant that during my days of clinical consulting, I would often engage in marital counselling and without doubt, it was this skill of 'Acknowledging Feelings' alone that could turn marriages around. Typically, the males were terrible at it, and the females yearned for it. When the males were brave enough to venture into this emotional arena, their women were delighted (and it's certainly true to say, that there were a good proportion of males who also longed for someone to listen to their emotions too).

5. Summarise

Summarising is when the listener attends to a broader range of events and information than in a straight paraphrase or acknowledging of feelings. It's simply pulling it all together. It's a re-cap.

In summarizing the other person's experience, the listener attempts to:
- Restate / repeat / reproduce
- Condense, and
- Clarify the other person's experience.

A summary covers a relatively longer time period (than, a paraphrase), eg., it puts together a number of statements, an entire phase of a session, or even an entire interview.

Summarizing serves **three** important functions:

(1) It helps **to crystallize** what the other person has been talking about. When the listener draws together both the feeling and content expressed throughout the conversation, the listener helps the other person to focus on the issues which most concern him or her.

(2) It serves **to stimulate** further talk on the issue, and at a potentially deeper level.

(3) It provides an opportunity for the listener to verify whether or not he or she is **perceiving** the other person correctly.

The Art of Asking Key Questions

What is it about questions that make them so important in any conversation let alone the conversations that leaders must engage in on a daily basis? You see, questions by their very nature, engage the other person. It's not like 'telling' or 'giving advice' where the other person can disregard what you have to say or simply tune you out.

Instead, a question entices people into the conversation. Asking a question means that the brain can't help itself. The brain is programmed and designed to find answers, fix 'stuff' and find solutions. That's its business. That's what it's good at. So, naturally enough when a question is asked, the brain immediately engages to try to find the answer.

Asking a question engages people. *But asking a powerful question engages powerfully.* So what is a powerful question? One that makes people think. You certainly know that you've asked a powerful question when the other person says, "That's a good question." What they mean is that your question is making them stop and think.

They are therefore thinking in a domain or area that they haven't considered before or they are having to reach into arenas where they need to consider options or viewpoints or actions that they haven't encountered before.

Asking a question and gaining a response means that you as a leader are also getting buy-in from the other.

At times, I have heard the opinion too that asking questions is somehow a sign of weakness in that the individual is supposed to know all the answers. Somehow, asking a question is apparently a reflection of incompetency. Not so.

However, effective leadership means that you need information and knowledge and the other person may have such information that is imperative to effective decision-making and critical to you doing your role. Asking questions elicits this kind of information.

"Leadership is not so much about knowing the right answers, as it is about knowing the right questions"

(Author unknown)

In my experience, what separates leaders from each other, is that the really successful ones have the ability to not only listen effectively, but to ask questions, yes, powerful questions.

Asking key questions and following up on what the other person has just said is a powerful way to gain empathy and understanding as well as show that you're really listening.

After all, you can't ask a question effectively if you're not listening.

- Often it can be helpful to ask clarifying questions eg., "Could you tell me more about that?" "What did you mean exactly when you said...?"
- Once you consider that you have heard ALL that needs to be said, ask, "What do you think is the most important aspect to what you've been saying?"
- "What do you think you'd like to do about what you've just said?" or "Is there anything you'd like to do about what you just said?"
- "Is there anything more that you'd like to add?"

If you had to ask only one question of your boss, staff, clients or customers, then it would be:
- *"What do you think?"*

When I led staff in my previous roles, I used to ask this question a good deal. The team knew that when they came to me with a question or an issue that they wanted an answer on, they knew the question that I would come back with first. As leaders in our organisations, it's up to us to coach colleagues and our staff through finding that answer. More often than not, when I asked this question, my team had a better answer than I did — or one that I hadn't thought about before. Once the other person has given a response, be prepared to listen intently and then ask further follow-up questions like "Anything else?"

The key really is to listen (using the skills listed above) and then ask simple follow-up questions. Classic questions in this regard are:
- "What do you mean by that?"
- "Tell me more."

Summary

As indicated previously, these key skills of listening and asking questions are covered in much more detail in my book "Listen up Now". Furthermore, this book has a series of homework exercises and practice sessions that helps you to refine your listening skills. I really do encourage you to either purchase a hard copy or else download the audio version of the book. You cannot be an effective leader without these skills.

Chapter 9 Summary
Communication

The Five Levels of Listening
There are actually five levels of listening ranging from ignoring and pretending through to empathic listening which is about really understanding what is being said and really understanding the feelings being expressed.

What is Listening?
The core components involve the following:
1. Empathy
2. Asking questions
3. Giving feedback
4. A learned skill

What It Is Not
It is not a whole bunch of things including maintaining a polite silence, having all the answers and giving advice, giving inappropriate minimal responses like "uh-huh" or "yes" or parroting back what you might have heard.

Why Don't We Listen
In essence, the failure to listen is really about our own egos taking over where we find it difficult to put ourselves aside where we give time, effort and energy to the other

person and where we concentrate on what they are saying with their story, their feelings and their thoughts.

The Art of Listening
Basically, there are **5 specific skills** that make up listening.
1. Stop and Look
2. Suspend Your Judgment
3. Paraphrase their Content
4. Acknowledge their Feelings
5. Summarise

The Art of Asking Key Questions
What separates some leaders from the really successful ones is the ability not only to listen effectively, but to ask questions, yes, powerful questions. Asking key questions and following up on what the other person has just said is a powerful way to gain empathy and understanding as well as show that you're really listening.

"Leaders who don't listen will eventually be surrounded by people who have nothing to say."

(John Reed Jnr)

CHAPTER 10

Coaching Others

The Case for Coaching

If your job is leading others, then the most important thing that you can do each day is to help your team members make progress at work that feels meaningful to them.

To do so, you must listen to each person and understand what drives them, help build connections between each person's work and the organisation's mission and strategic objectives, provide timely feedback and help each person learn to grow on an ongoing basis.

Regularly communicating about their development and having coaching conversations is essential. In fact, it is now clear from the research available, that the single most important managerial competency that separates highly effective managers from average ones is coaching.

"I absolutely believe that people, unless coached, never reach their maximum potential."

(Bob Nardelli)

Sadly though, as Julia Milner and Trenton Milner point out in the *Harvard Business Review* (August 14, 2018), most managers think that they are coaching, when in fact, they are not. They are simply giving advice, telling others what to do or mentoring (those distinctions are outlined below).

However, coaching is quickly becoming one of the leading tools and strategies that successful people are using in order to enhance their lives further and allow them to lead extraordinary lives. According to IBISWorld in 2017 in an article headed, *"Life Coaches: Market Research Report"*, life coaching (as distinct from executive or leadership coaching), is growing at nearly 5% per year. So, not only are individuals turning to coaching to develop their lives, but it is imperative that leaders and managers now need to learn this skill in order to be effective at what they do.

What is Coaching?

Someone once said, *"Coaching is like having a personal trainer for your life"*.

What is a coach exactly? A coach was originally a form of transport and first used around 1556. It was defined as..."*A coach transports a valued person from where they are to where they want to be"* (Old Webster Dictionary).

Interesting notion. In other words, coaching unlocks a person's potential to maximise his/her own performance. It helps them learn rather than teaching them (Centre for Creative Leadership).

"When looking to enhance knowledge and ability, even the most elite and talented athletes need a coach, someone who will help them analyse their performance and set goals for what they want to achieve in the future, and direction in achieving those goals. Business is no different." (Rebecca Spicer, "The Coaching Drill", Dynamic Business, July 2007).

A coach therefore is a *"trusted role model, advisor, wise person, friend, Mensch, steward or guide -- a person who works with emerging human and organisational forces to tap new energy and purpose, to shape new visions and plans, and to generate desired results. A coach is someone trained and devoted to* *guiding others into increased competence, commitment and confidence"* (F. Hudson, Handbook of Coaching, 1999).

Finally, **let's understand the differences...a ONE sentence Vignette**...

- **Mentor:** Show you the way
- **Therapist:** Follow the trail of tears
- **Consultant:** Follow the expert advice
- **Trainer:** Follow the instruction
- **Coach:** Follow the trail of dreams

For further information on these distinctions, please visit:

https://crossways.com.au/coaching/coaching-explained/

What are the Keys to Coaching?

Mindset

It's your headspace. It all comes down to what you believe and who you are at your core. What is your essence? Are you an ego and it's all about you, or are you more soul-filled and others-oriented? Do you really care about others? Are you prepared to give people the personal gift of time? As the saying goes, *"People do not care what you know until they know that you care."*

Look below for example, at the different kinds of beliefs that "Bosses" might hold in contrast to "Coaches".

Beliefs that Bosses Hold	Beliefs that Coaches Hold
Their job is to push people or drive them.	They are there to lift and support people.
They talk at people by telling, directing and lecturing.	They engage in dialogue with people by asking, requesting and listening.
They control others through the decisions they make.	They facilitate others to make decisions and empower them to implement their own decisions.
They know the answers.	They believe they must seek the answers.
They trigger insecurity through administering a healthy dose of fear as an effective way to achieve compliance.	They believe in using purpose to inspire commitment and stimulate creativity.
They believe that their job is to point out errors.	They believe that their job is to celebrate learning.
They believe in solving problems and making decisions.	They believe in facilitating others to solve problems and make decisions.
They believe in delegating responsibility.	They believe in modelling accountability.

They create structure and procedures for people to follow.	They create vision and promote flexibility through values as guidelines for behaviour.
They believe in doing things right.	They believe in doing the right things.
They believe that their power lies in their knowledge.	They believe that the power lies in their vulnerability.
They focus on the bottom line.	The focus on the process that creates the bottom-line result.

(Adapted from Thomas Crane, "Becoming a Coach for the
Teams you Lead", in *Coaching for Leadership* edited by
Marshall Goldsmith; 2000).

Do you see the difference? Do you see what it takes to come full around from a "boss" philosophy to a "coach" philosophy? This is a fundamental shift in what it means to be a leader. This new perspective is absolutely imperative if you really want to join that throng of new leaders who are putting aside beliefs and practices from the past in order to come into the new world order in terms of leadership.

Solution-Focused

The most powerful position from which to observe and interact with others is the solution-focus in comparison with a focus on problem-orientation. The solution focus is a fantastic vantage-point and allows you to use effective questioning to facilitate the sorts of conversations and relationships that can make a real difference to the way things are done and the mood in which they are done.

The following table contrasts the solution-focus with a focus on problems or difficulties:

Problem Focus	Solution Focus
Assessing problems	Clarifying goals
"Can you tell me about the problem?"	"What do you want to change?"
Awareness of recent impairment	Awareness of recent improvement
"What went wrong last week?"	"How did you cope so well last week?"
Explaining problems	Explaining progress
"Is lack of progress a symptom of something deeper?"	"Have we clarified the central issue or goal?"
Highlighting weaknesses & failures	Highlighting strengths & resources

Discovering what works and doing more of it is generally a positive, enjoyable and empowering activity for all concerned. Whether you are a teacher, a manager, a parent, a friend or a coach, you will reap benefits for your students, staff, children, friends, clients and yourself.

Cultivating the seeds of what is already going well helps to reap positive change for all concerned. You can nurture the growth of positive change through small "germinating" events. This means that people need only capitalise on and increase the percentage of their time spent doing what is already working – this has benefits in time, cost and effort. This form of change takes the path of least resistance.

Asking "when does success happen already?" generates a different kind of conversation from "when do things go wrong?" Energy, enthusiasm and cooperation are frequent and welcome side-effects of the solution-focus.

Can Coaching be Learned?

Yes, but is very much a personal journey. As David Hale explains in his PhD thesis (2008) titled, *"Development of a Validated Core Competency Skill Set for Executive Coaches"*, a coach can be developed if he or she possess **the passion and desire**, but he makes the point that *the training is more of a personal journey than simply educational attainment.*

This though is the rub. Are managers and executives really up for the journey? A personal journey? Are you up for it?

Sure, you are no doubt a very competent person who may have gained a trade of some sort before moving up the ranks or may have gained a professional degree or diploma in your chosen field before becoming a supervisor or manager at some stage. No doubt you are technically very good because the leadership role is now yours.

Now however, you are being asked to go on a coaching journey as a way of enhancing your leadership and management skills. Skills is one thing, but a personal journey is another.

This falls well outside the "Comfort zone" of most and right into what can be called the "Courage zone". See my video on this topic:

https://www.youtube.com/watch?v=pCMEQ1EhuA8

Hale then goes on to say that skills are teachable and learnable, and techniques may be replicated, but true understanding and proficiency only comes from **carefully honed practice in real-world situations.**

Understand though that in the coaching course that I run for team leaders, managers and executives, it is in fact, a 12-month program to really understand and practice the coaching skills required. It is not a 1 or 2-day workshop! Could you ever learn to be really good at something after one or two days of instruction and then probably have no follow up? To really understand the program that I teach, see the following:

https://leadershipcoaching.com.au/leadership-coach-training/the-abn-group-as-a-case-study/

That is not meant to discourage you in any way, but simply to highlight that regardless of the skills you wish to master, such as cooking, golfing, sewing, drawing and so on, it takes time and real effort.

Coaching in a very real sense then, is no different than learning any other skill – you actually have to do it.

The hard truth is this – that every coach learns through doing. And "doing" is a verb, an action word, not a noun.

What are the Skills?

We have already covered the key core elements of coaching, namely, **listening and asking key questions**. As mooted above, if you can't get these skills mastered, then being an effective leader is virtually impossible. If you can't master these skills, then you can also forget about being a manager-coach. It just won't happen.

So, presuming that you've mastered **the skills of listening** (or are in the process of getting these skills under your belt as it were), then there is a structured way to have a coach conversation with your team and possibly your peers.

It's called **GRO-DOH**. I created this model for coaching based on a series of credentialed coach courses that I undertook in California (USA). Let me outline this framework.

Goal: This is a critical first step. This is where you agree on the topic for discussion. It might be a short-term issue or could be a longer term objective. Nevertheless, it is absolutely critical that both the coach-manager as well as the staff member agree on the topic to be covered. This provides both focus and agreement so that both parties know exactly what is being discussed.

Key questions might be:

- *"What would you like to take away from this discussion?"*
- *"What is the issue that you'd like to focus on?"*
- *"What would you like to be different after this session?"*
- *"What outcome would you like from this discussion?"*

Reality: At this point, the individual team member might provide some history, some self-assessment, or provide feedback (or indeed, the coach-manager may ask about these areas). Overall, it is important for the manager or leader to understand the overall picture that has or is occurring, to avoid or check any assumptions being made, and to discard any irrelevant history.

Key questions for example might be;

- *"What is the current situation?"*
- *"Tell me more about the circumstance?"*
- *"How do you know that this is accurate?"*
- *"When does this happen? How often?"*
- *"How do others see this situation?"*
- *"What other factors are relevant?"*
- *"What have you tried? What worked?"*

Options: This is where the manager or leader invites suggestions for possible solutions from the team member rather than jump in with well-intended advice or instruction. It's critical that the coach-manager invites suggestions first, and once the full range of options might have been covered, the manager can then feel free to offer their own solutions (if they had any).

Key questions to ask include;

- *"What has worked for you in the past?"*
- *"What are all the possible actions that you can see?"*
- *"What are some potential pitfalls?"*
- *"What do you think should be done?"*
- *"What is the benefit of that idea?"*
- *"What would have to happen to make it work?"*

Direct Action: This is where a decision is made to select a particular option and act on that option.

Key questions are;
- *"What option will you choose to act on?"*
- *"What steps will you now take?"*
- *"By when will you do this?"*
- *"What will you do to get the support you need to move along?"*

Obstacles: Having committed to a key action (or actions), it's important to identify any possible obstacles that might get in the road and then discuss ways around such obstacles.

Key questions for instance, could include;
- *"Do you see any obstacles?"*
- *"What might stop you or get in the way?"*
- *"How can you overcome this?"*
- *"How will you know that you're on track for success?"*

Homework: This is the final step in the process which is a kind of wrap-up where the actions being taken are summarised and the timing is reinforced.

Further key questions to ask could include;
- *"What support do you need to make it all happen?"*
- *"When will you check back with me?"*
- *"When will we catch up again?"*

This model for having a coaching conversation has been of major benefit to countless managers and leaders who have used this approach when staff members have come to them with issues or questions, or when perhaps the manager themselves has had an issue that they wish to bring up with a team member.

Chapter 10 Summary
Coaching Others

The Case for Coaching
It is now clear from the research available, that the single most important managerial competency that separates highly effective managers and leaders from average ones is coaching.

What are the Keys to Coaching?
Mindset
It all comes down to what you believe and who you are at your core. What is your essence? Are you an ego and it's all about you, or are you more soul-filled and others-oriented? Do you really care about your people? Are you prepared to give people the personal gift of your time and effort?

Solution-Focused
Rather than concentrating on what went wrong and why, and focusing on weaknesses and faults and who was to blame, a more effective way of coming to grips with issues is to focus instead on possible solutions, ways to prevent the issue from happening again and working on strengths and resources that are available.

Can Coaching be Learned?

The training in becoming a coach is more of a personal journey than simply just educational attainment or achievement. "Personal" because it requires the leader to be vulnerable and step into the "Courage Zone" to be willing to learn an entirely new set of skills. The skills are teachable and learnable, and techniques may be replicated, but true understanding and proficiency only comes from **carefully honed practice in real-world situations.**

What are the Skills?

The key core elements of coaching are **listening and asking key questions**. As mooted previously, if you can't get these skills mastered, then being an effective leader is virtually impossible. If you can't master these skills, then you can also forget about being a manager-coach.

Add to these core skills is the **GRO-DOH Model** which is a framework for how to conduct a structured coach conversation.

CHAPTER 11

Being Assertive and Delegating

These are important skills to have when you're a leader. How else can you really lead? Yet, many new leaders struggle to be assertive with their team members and struggle to delegate out work. Why is this so?

In my opinion, there are two primary factors and they are called "Drivers". A driver is a script or theme that you have learnt early in life because it worked for you as a child and you continue to use those scripts or programs as you grow up. In other words, it continues to drive you.

However, ironically, as an adult they actually can sabotage you. As a leader, they sink you. So, what are those primary drivers.

The Driver to Please Others

Somehow, some of us learn very early in life that in order to get along, to get rewards and to survive in the world, the best thing to do was to please other people especially people who were significant in our life like parents, grandparents and later, teachers and others. Get them to like us was our motto! Keep others happy by giving in to their needs, their wants and their desires. Then they'll like us and we'll be OK and life will be good!

Now, we didn't consciously make this decision, but at a subconscious level, we worked out that that's how we needed to survive as a child in order to get by. Further, this driver served us well in adolescence where we made sure (consciously and sub-consciously) to get on with others including our teachers. We didn't muck up, we got our work done and we generally toed the line. People seemed to like us as a result.

Take this to the extreme, however, and you end up pleasing others so much that you never (or rarely) end up pleasing yourself.

In a sense, people whittle themselves away. When people do this, they not only feel down and depressed, but they feel inadequate because they have successfully sabotaged themselves. They don't know who they really are because they have never allowed themselves the chance to consider themselves or to be their own person ("What if they don't like me? That would be terrible.").

They are lost to themselves. They don't know their strengths or talents and "what makes them tick". They haven't discovered what makes them unique, what makes them them!

"We'd be less concerned with what others thought of us if we knew how seldom they actually do."

(Chinese Proverb)

Certainly, it is fitting and appropriate to please others and help them, but to do so **all or most** of the time, to the continual detriment of yourself, is not wise. Continually pleasing others frequently means that you end up having nothing left for yourself. No time, no energy, nothing.

Starting to stand up for yourself and therefore having people say "no" to you might be the unthinkable. "Oh, how awful!" "How embarrassing." If someone says "no" to you, you take it personally. We don't like people to 'reject' us in any way.

Imagine then how this might impact you as a new leader. You find it difficult to tell others what to do, to confront others if necessary, to set targets, to set deadlines, and to be assertive. You may not delegate out work because that might somehow "impose" on others and they may not "like you". Failure to delegate means that you end up with the work piling up on your plate and in the end, you feel swamped with so much work. Of course, this workload means that you have no time either, to attend to your team. You're drowning in work.

You also tend not to speak up if you see some issue occurring like a staff member not performing well or perhaps two team members not getting on well together. You struggle with controlling your team and often new leaders just "hope" that the issues will go away (they don't, and in fact, they get worse). The team tends to become discouraged because there is little, if any, direction, and perhaps one or two more "rebellious" team members might push limits (eg., turn up late for meetings, don't produce work on time), or else one or two members engage in gossip and innuendo and before too long, the team is toxic. If the new leader struggled before, now at this point, they are literally drowning. All because they were too afraid to speak up and intervene.

"Why try to please everyone? The reality is that around 3 out of every 10 people are not going to like you anyway!"

(Darryl Cross)

Because of your need to please, you may well get pulled in to all sorts of meetings, projects and activities including the social club at work. You can't really say "no" which means that you're stretched in all sorts of ways and often end up running from meeting to meeting. At the end of the day you're exhausted and wonder what you really did in your day. Of course, this might also mean that you need to stay back to try to get on top of your workload. Life ends up going to work, eating and going to sleep before the cycle repeats itself next day.

When Sammy Davis Junior was on tour in Australia, he was asked, "What is the secret to success?" He replied, "I don't know, but what I do know is the secret to failure – it's trying to please everyone else."

Not surprisingly, the new leader experiences anxiety which moves into feelings of being depressed. Physically, they start to experience fatigue and tiredness and perhaps become ill or sick because of the stress of it all.

The overall message is **what got you here, won't get you there.** In other words, your need to please others might have worked as a child and into young adulthood, but it now no longer serves you and will in fact sabotage you if you wish to stay in the leadership role.

You need to decide that if you want to grow personally and grow professionally into leadership, then you have to change this pattern at both the conscious and sub-conscious level. You have to move into the courage zone and be prepared to do it differently. I have written much more about this topic in the book called *"Stopping your Self-sabotage: Steps to Increasing Your Self-confidence"* which is available in either hard copy, kindle or audio.

www.HowtoStopSelfSabotage.com

The Driver to Be Perfect

Again, this driver originates from very early days when as a child you learnt that in order to get any praise you had to do things well. Very well. It wasn't good enough to do a good job, it had to be perfect. This carried over to school where you had to achieve well and get top marks (or close to it). It might have been on the sports field where you had to be in the best players each week or be in the top goal scorers. It might have been in the gym class where you had to win at the competitions or get in the medals. Nevertheless, the message was clear, to get on and to get recognition, you had to do it perfectly.

As before, this theme continued on through school and into trade school or university and then into your first job. The way to handle life is to try to be perfect in what you do. It got you rewards. You might have gotten awards at school or for your studies, and at work, your bosses would have loved you because you did the job exceptionally well. If you do a really, really good job, you'll be accepted and others will like you. As a perfectionist, you would hate to make a mistake or have someone criticize you ("How dreadful." "How awful." "How humiliating.").

Although they strive relentlessly for perfection, these people always feel inferior because they never quite reach the perfection they want. It's never good enough. This is, in fact, a dead-end. Certainly, too, it's rarely good enough for those around them who frequently find fault which just compounds the situation.

It's a no-win situation in which they have successfully sabotaged themselves. They try not to make mistakes and try hard to get things right all the time. They lack the spontaneity and freedom to experiment and be themselves. They experience real stress. They are under constant duress.

The message, instead, is that life is about making mistakes and learning from them. This is how people grow and develop. It might seem strange, but those who have been the most successful in life are those who have made the most mistakes and learnt from them.

"The only failure in life is the failure to participate."

(Author unknown)

Are you prepared to get it "close enough", and do a conscientious job without doing it perfectly? Have you ever noticed that what you think is "perfect" may not be what the next person considers "perfect"? Being perfect therefore is a no-win.

Imagine then how this might impact you as a new leader. While before you had control over your work and you did a really good job at it (often because you stayed behind after work or came in on weekends to catch up), your team members probably don't have the same standards as you do. As a perfectionist, you were able to control your own work, but now with people in your team, there are so many other factors at play which makes control extremely difficult.

How do you manage this? Typically, you might decide to do all the work yourself or at least check all the work before it goes out which means you become inundated. You might get behind as a result, and of course, none of this is 'perfect' and it sends you into a depressed spiral. You probably don't want to come to work or have sick days off (because you might be genuinely sick or just want some reprieve somehow).

"It's not who you are that holds you back, it is who you think you are not."

(Author unknown)

Now imagine if you had both drivers (pleasing others and being prefect) inherent in your upbringing.

It's really not hard to imagine the stress that builds up very quickly for a new leader. They get out of their depth very quickly. They feel overwhelmed and isolated; it must be them that is at fault; obviously they're not good enough; maybe they weren't cut out for this management stuff anyway; their confidence plummets; they feel trapped.

Stress in the form of anxiety or depression becomes obvious and ultimately, if the new leader doesn't make some changes, they end up either burning out (which is tragic to see where the repercussions are serious in terms of their personality and future career prospects) or they end up stepping back from leadership and staying in their former role with no responsibility for others. I have seen both occur. At least in the latter circumstance, there is no damage to their "psyche".

As I've said above, what got you here, won't get you there. Again, for a more in-depth analysis, I'd refer you to my other book *"How to Stop Your Self-sabotage"*.

Being Assertive

Presuming that you have taken steps on re-working those sabotaging drivers, let's focus now on the skill of assertion itself.

Beliefs

In order to be assertive, it is important to accept two basic beliefs about standing up for yourself. These include:

- That assertion (rather than manipulation, submission, or hostility) enriches life and ultimately leads to more satisfying personal relationships with people.
- That everyone is entitled to act assertively and to express honest thoughts, feelings, and beliefs.

Steps of Behaviour

So what happens if you decide to be appropriately assertive? If you're feeling stretched, tense and under pressure, how can you respond next time you receive a request to do something? How can you appropriately confront a team member about a specific issue? What do you say if there is yet another request to attend a meeting which is really for information only and one that only keeps you in the loop.

Note the following pointers:

- You don't have to respond with an answer immediately. Don't be caught off-guard. Give yourself time. Say something like, *"It's nice of you to ask me, but I'd like to think about it for a day (a week)."* In the ensuing day or week, you can usually sort out your priorities and decide if you really want to be involved.

- When responding to the request and you need to say "no", be definite and say something like: *"Thank you for thinking of me, but I don't wish to be involved at this stage."* And if the other person persists? Simply repeat what you've already said – don't be conned into giving endless excuses and reasons and having to justify yourself.

There are other times though when being assertive is necessary and you need to stand up for yourself. For example, what about when someone pushes in front of you in the queue or a workmate uses your desk and leaves it in a mess or a team member is repeatedly late with deadlines?

A **useful formula or guide** for helping you to assertively express difficult negative feelings is to use the following phrases:

"When .... (objectively describe the other's behaviour) .... *the effects are* .... (describe how the other's behaviour concretely affects your life or feelings) .... *I feel* .... (describe your feelings) .... *and I'd prefer....*" (describe what you want instead).

For example;

"When you use my desk, you leave it in a mess and it's difficult for me to get down to work again and I feel annoyed about that, so I'd prefer if you

either didn't use it or cleaned it up once you'd used it."

"When you continually miss deadlines, then you not only let yourself down and others in the team, but it means that the Unit as a whole looks bad and it puts me under stress too, so I'd really like you to meet the deadlines from this point onward."

If you can risk being assertive, you will be your own best friend -- you will learn to really like yourself and you won't feel resentful towards others or want to hide every time a friend, work colleague or team member makes a request of you. You will also feel free to accept invitations to be involved in those areas where you really wish to help and consider that you have something to offer.

Delegating Effectively

Delegation is the work of a leader if you really want to get things done. For many managers though, the hardest part of delegating is trusting that a task will be done well. But it becomes easier when you think of it as a chance to train your staff – not just get rid of some work.

The next time you need to delegate something, start by determining who on your team is ready to handle more responsibility. Then create simple tasks to help them learn the skills they'll need. If you'd like someone to take over running a weekly meeting for instance, have them practice each part of the process; one week, they can create an agenda, which you'll review. The next, they can watch you run the meeting, with plenty of chances to ask questions. Eventually they'll be ready to try running the meeting themselves, after which you can offer feedback.

This kind of teaching can be time-consuming, but it will go a long way toward preparing your team for more-complex work. So, keep in mind that delegation is really about teaching or training others.

Beliefs

In order to delegate, it is important to hold certain beliefs about delegation such as:

- Understand the importance of delegating to others as a way to offload work and get more done in your busy life.
- Understand that delegation is important in helping others grow and develop and it all serves to increase self-confidence in others.

Levels of Delegation

There are actually six main ways to delegate and you may use any one of these at particular times:

1. *"Do as I say"* – here the instruction is more of a directive and is probably for the junior team member who lacks specific skills and who may be somewhat hesitant or not motivated.

2. *"Look into this"* – this is an exploratory request where you may want certain information or you may be testing the team member to ascertain their level of skill and ability or their general commitment.

3. *"Give me your advice and then I'll decide"* – here you are giving some responsibility to do the research or project and you're seeking an opinion, but you're also letting the team member know that you'll make the final decision (because you may want to test their decision-making ability, or in fact, you may need to make the decision yourself because of the magnitude or repercussions of the decision).

4. *"Explore, decide and check with me"* – this is where you are prepared to give more responsibility to the team member, but want to oversee the final decision being made.

5. *"Explore and decide within these limits"* – here the accountability is clear and the team member knows the parameters (eg., financial constraints) in which they can move.

6. *"Take care of it for me"* – ultimate responsibility and accountability is handed over to the team member.

"The secret of success is not in doing your own work but in recognising the right person to do it."

(Andrew Carnegie)

Steps of Behaviour

There are a number of steps to be undertaken so that you can effectively delegate:

1. Introduce the task; work out what needs to be delegated. What is the task?

2. Choose the right person; work out their strengths and weakness, their interests and what their current workload looks like. Can they handle the task and can it be done in the time frame given their present workload? Would this task or project help develop them as an individual?

3. Communicate clearly what you want done; state what you're looking for at the end. Specify what you want it to look like when it's completed and done well. Specify the time-frame that is required.

4. Ensure understanding; get them to repeat back to you what you believe that you have said. Ask them if they need clarification on anything. Get their commitment to the task and the time-frame.

5. Collaboratively work out the methods for follow up; set up a reporting and communication system so you know how things are progressing. This is a critical step in that so many leaders delegate and just expect it to happen. You need to track the progress of what is occurring and be available to offer assistance if necessary.

This skill like so many others gets easier the more times that you do it. The keys though are clear communication and deliberate follow up. I have seen so many leaders come undone because they took it for granted that the project was being done or they assumed that the staff member had it under control only to find out at the last minute that it was well behind schedule or that there were holes in it somehow.

If this occurs, you look poor as a leader not only to your team, but to other units or departments and to your boss all who may be relying on the task being done.

"If you want to do a few small things right, do them yourself. If you want to do great things and make an impact, learn to delegate."

(John C Maxwell)

Chapter 11 Summary
Being Assertive and Delegating

The Driver to Please Others
Somehow, some of us learn very early in life that in order to get along, to get rewards and to survive in the world, the best thing to do was to please other people especially people who were significant in our life like parents, grandparents and later, teachers and others. Take this to the extreme, however, and you end up pleasing others so much that you never (or rarely) end up pleasing yourself.

The Driver to Be Perfect
Again, this driver originates from very early days when as a child you learnt that in order to get any praise you had to do things well. Very well. It wasn't good enough to do a good job, it had to be perfect. As a perfectionist, you would hate to make a mistake or have someone criticise you ("How dreadful." "How awful." "How humiliating.").

Now imagine if you had both drivers (pleasing others and being prefect) inherent in your upbringing. It's really not hard to imagine the stress that builds up very quickly for a new leader. They get out of their depth very quickly because they fail to delegate effectively ("What if they get upset with my delegating some stuff to them and what if they don't do it perfectly like I would?") and they resist being assertive and saying it straight ("What if they get annoyed with me and don't like me?").

Being Assertive

The skill of being assertive relies on two fundamental beliefs that are necessary plus there is a verbal script to follow which gives a recipe for being assertive.

Delegating Effectively

Again, there are certain beliefs that you need to hold in order to be effective at delegation and then there are the procedural steps to follow to ensure that delegation occurs and that importantly, follow up actually happens.

CHAPTER 12

Dealing with Conflict

There is absolutely no doubt in my mind that this is the one area that terrifies most managers and leaders. Over a number of decades of coaching, it is by far the most common conversation that I have, and it's about how to manage conflict. It is the one area that leaders will lie awake at night worrying about. They lose sleep over it. They feel anxious and at times nauseas. They often lose their appetite or experience diarrhea. They put it off. They hope it will all go away.

"95% of conflict is over opinions and feelings rather than facts."

(Author unknown)

The reality is that conflict and difficult people are inevitable anywhere you go. It would probably be more peaceful if it was not the case – but the fact is, **if you only put two people on the same planet, sooner or later they would tread on each other's toes**, if only by accident.

The frequency of having to deal with difficult people varies enormously, and some unfortunate individuals are forced to tolerate an almost continuously hostile environment.

Individuals react in a variety of ways, countering aggression with aggression, or alternatively withdrawing, becoming depressed and/or excessively anxious.

Hostility exists because people (at work, home, and play) are competing for promotion, remuneration, and power because of the personalities involved.

The reasons for people being difficult, aggressive and angry are complex, but not very helpful for a leader who is trying to deal with a hostile or difficult person.

---

*"I am at peace with God. My conflict
is with man."*

(Charlie Chapman)

Another problem is that at work for example, you do not choose the people that you work with or the customers/clients/patients who come to you. **Often, we are thrust into an organisation or group where we have to work or relate to people whom we would normally try to avoid.**

So what are the formulas for handling this obviously difficult area of leadership? Let's look at some scenarios.

Team Member Comes to You all Fired Up

There are a number of steps involved and if you remember to follow them, then the chances are that you will successfully manage that staff member who comes to you with an issue especially if they seem tense, annoyed or visibly angry or perhaps sad or overwhelmed. You could in fact, rightfully use the GRO-DOH model here too (see Chapter 10, Page 151), if you wished, in that such a framework works well in conflictual situations. Nevertheless, see the steps below.

1. Put Your *Protective Shield* Up
This is not the time to respond immediately, and instead, you need to steady and prepare yourself. Immediately try to picture or imagine a protective shield surrounding you before you respond. Perhaps take a deep breath and pause. Maybe visualise yourself stepping back from the team member's comment and giving yourself some space. This is critical because it buys you a few seconds to examine your critic or your staff

member's intentions. Should you explore the criticism further as a possible way to grow professionally or personally? Or should you dismiss it as only a hurtful message? Where is this message coming from? What's the agenda here?

2. Remain *Calm* – DO NOT GET DEFENSIVE

If necessary, try to look poker-faced. Don't allow the team member to think that they have caught you off-guard or off-balance.

3. Stop, Look, and *Listen*

As has been indicated above, this is the number 1 rule in the list of listening skills (see Chapter 9, Page 127). Give the person your undivided attention. Turn away from the computer screen so you're not distracted. Stop what you're doing and look at them.

4. *Paraphrase* what they just said

Again, this is a critical listening skill (see how important listening is in all sorts of situations).

5. If they are not happy with what you just said, *paraphrase it again* until you get it right

6. Don't block the *Communication*

• Don't judge or give an opinion.

• Don't prematurely give a quick solution (this is a sure-fire way to kill the conversation in that a quick fix may be the wrong solution, and besides, it says that you really haven't heard the full story and it smacks a tad of being defensive because you're rushing to get it over and done with; it will probably also inflame the situation).

• Don't dodge the issue and talk about an allied situation or try to placate the person which also smacks of being defensive.

7. Put yourself in their *shoes* – try to see it from their angle

This is called empathy. Seeing the situation from their perspective. Remember, this conversation is not about you; it's about them.

8. Ask *Questions*

Again, a key listening skill. Ask questions to clarify what they might have said to really ensure that you've heard exactly what they wish to say. Ask questions to get more of the history of the situation.

9. Restate the *Problem*

Make sure again that you're on target.

10. Now seek *a Solution*

Either ask them for what they think will solve the matter or provide a solution yourself (but offer it tentatively) or say that both you and them ought to think about it and make another time to discuss.

11. Find a point of *Agreement* if possible – could be simply arranging the next meeting time

12. Respond visibly with *Action* – write something down, make a call, etc.

13. Restate or summarise what *Action* can be taken to handle this situation

These are the steps that will ensure that you don't inflame the situation or make it worse in any way. These simple steps will allow you the opportunity to dissolve the tension and seek about finding a collaborative solution.

"Conflict when handled correctly, strengthens."

(Benjamin Watson)

You go to the Team Member with an Issue

How do you communicate in a straightforward genuine manner without creating defensiveness or hostility from the staff member? How can you discuss with the team member in such a way that you do not intentionally offend them? Professor Kim Cameron in his 2013 book titled, *"Practicing Positive Leadership"* provided an important distinction.

One of the most important attributes of being supportive in your communication is the ability to be *descriptive* rather than *evaluative* in the delivery of the message.

In other words, **evaluative communication** gives a judgment, provides an opinion, or places a label on individuals or their behaviour. For example, comments such as, "You did it all wrong" or "It's your fault" or "You are ineffective" are all evaluative in style. They do not suspend judgement. They are generally critical and fault finding.

Needless to say, individuals who receive such evaluative statements generally feel attacked and tend to retreat and become defensive or occasionally aggressive or hostile. Naturally enough, they push back and defend themselves by proclaiming that they are not wrong or it was not their fault or that they are very capable as individuals.

In contrast, **descriptive comments** are more objective in kind and allow the leader to be more congruent and authentic in the delivery of the message. Descriptive communication involves three steps:
1. Describe the event, behaviour, or circumstance objectively
2. Describe outcomes and/or feelings and not the other person's attributes
3. Suggest alternative solutions that could resolve the issue

When you have to say something you don't think someone else, including a team member, will enjoy hearing, be brief, use carefully worded "I statements" (not "you" comments) and relax by being prepared. If you wish to really think through the issue and get your thoughts straight, then please see **Appendix 5** ("Preparing an Issue for Discussion").

Try this step-by-step sequence *(Note: **Steps 1 to 4** are all said in one whole statement):*

Step 1: Describe how you feel about starting the discussion.
> *"I am   .... about discussing this, because
> ...."*

Examples:
> *"I am hesitant about discussing this because I don't
> want you to get this out of proportion."*
> *"I'm reticent about discussing this because I don't
> want you to get it out of perspective"*
> *OR*
> *"I'd like to talk to you about something – will this time
> work?"*
> *"Can I give you some feedback?"*

It's important how you start the conversation. It needs to be done in such a way as to flag that there is a serious side to what you're about to say. Most leaders don't know how to start a conversation when they are about to give negative feedback. They might go "softly softly" and talk about the weather or the latest sports results, and if they do that, then how on earth do they turn the conversation around to get to where they want to go?

Further, engaging in polite chatter first up is a kind of deceptive way to begin and I've certainly heard team members get annoyed that they were called into the boss' office and it was all "paly paly" and then they had "a bomb" dropped on them.

Step 2: Describe what happened.
"When I (saw or heard) ……………………….. "
Example:
"When I see you come into the meeting late and then roll your eyes at what others are saying…"

It is important, as indicated above, to be able to clearly describe the behavior that is obvious and can be seen or heard. It then doesn't become your opinion or evaluative in nature.

However, please note that because most individuals will not act up in front of the boss, you as the leader, may only get to learn about any poor behavior through hearsay. *It's important then to act on that hearsay.* If you happen to be wrong in your 'hearsay', it still gives the team member the opportunity to clarify what is going on and give their explanation. Even if they deny the apparent 'hearsay' (although it might be true), it sends a clear message that you are aware of what is going on. Generally though, in my experience, where there is smoke there is fire.

Step 3: Describe what effect it had on you and others.
"Then I (assumed, felt, had to) ………………….. "

Example:
"Then it impacted the others in the group with some getting upset and others getting annoyed..."
Again, stay with what you observed and what you saw or heard (even if it is hearsay).

Step 4: Describe what you would like now (and indicate a willingness to compromise).
Example: *"What I'd like now is ....[state the solution]... ,* **but maybe there is something I haven't thought of or that I've missed."**
(Now stop and wait for their response.)

Note that this section above in bold is important because it provides a willingness to compromise as well as being a qualifier in that it is possible that you may, in fact, have missed or overlooked something.

Other examples:
"Next time, I'd like to see ...[solution]... happen."
"What thoughts do you have on how this might be resolved?"
"How can we prevent this from happening again?"
"Instead, can you do..."

Step 5: Listen carefully to their response
This is a critical time where you really need to use your listening skills. Drill down and enquire further if necessary by asking key questions. Take your time to really understand what is going on.

- Inquire into the team member's views.
- Use paraphrasing, acknowledgment of their feelings and summarising.
- Do a perception check.
- Dig for full understanding; don't be satisfied with the surface response. Often, they may try to fob you off, so ask further questions.
- Make sure your staff member knows that you fully understand and acknowledge his or her position and interests.

Step 6: If they become defensive

It is possible that the team member might push back in any number of ways, but if you simply use your listening skills and continue to ask questions, then you can stay in control of the conversation. Sometimes, the staff member might:

...get hostile,

...demand who told you these things,

...ask questions and push back,

...debate the issue,

...cry or withdraw.

It is important not to be put off. Sometimes these particular ploys are manipulative and other times they might be genuine. Just use your reflective listening techniques and stay with the issue. Listening is key here.

Step 7: Push for a Solution / Outcome

If necessary, keep repeating your solution or outcome (unless of course the team member or the both of you come up with a better one). *Set a time when the situation will be reviewed again.* This might be in one or two week's time, but should be no longer than three weeks if at all possible. It's called accountability and it serves to ensure that there is a review time and that the conversation just wasn't a "one hit wonder" or a "flash in the pan" as it were.

Team Member with a Mental Health Issue

How do you approach a team member whom you suspect might have a mental health issue? In my experience, most managers and leaders tend to shy away from mental health issues for a number of reasons. First, they actually don't know what to do and secretly just hope that it all goes away. Second, they are afraid of exacerbating the issue or somehow making it worse. "What if" statements run through their head ("What if they had a 'nervous breakdown' after I spoke to them?" "What if they then went off and suicided?") which all means they put off approaching a staff member.

"People do not care what you know until they know that you care."

(Author unknown)

The major mental health issues are generally going to be either anxiety or depression and sometimes anger. Occasionally, there might be alcoholism, gambling addiction, bi-polar disorder, borderline personality disorder, obsessive compulsive disorder and perhaps a combination of these in some form.

Irrespective, I have outlined the common red-flags or tell-tale signs that are easy to spot in another book titled, *"The Dark Clouds at Work"* which is available in either hard copy, kindle or audio at the following website:

https://depressionatwork.com

The recipe for what to do with a probable mental health issue could follow these lines.

1. **Observe**; clearly most managers and leaders have little difficulty in recognising that specific staff members might be "off their game" or "not themselves lately". For depressives for instance, that might look like; decreased energy and productivity, inability to concentrate, forgetfulness, inability to organise or delegate tasks, making frequent mistakes, absenteeism, and maybe problems with other staff members in a lack of cooperation or conflict.

2. **Offer Feedback**; find a private occasion to talk to them and tell them what you've noticed and then ask if anything is wrong or if they are really okay. It is important to say what you've seen

because this gives extra credibility to the question about how they might be doing. It also shows that you care. It's also important that such feedback is given in a constructive, non-threatening way.

"I've noticed lately that you seem very sluggish and look tired and your dress-sense has dropped off, so I wondering how you're going right now?"

"I've been aware that you don't come to our happy hours or birthday lunches any more. Is everything alright?"

"I've noticed that you seem more short and abrupt than you used to be, and I'm wondering what might be going on with you?"

3.   **Listen**; use your listening skills and tune in to what they might say. Try to understand their perspective, paraphrase what they say, and repeat it back to them. Use statements such as, *"What you're saying is..."* or, *"What I heard you say was..."* Perhaps too they could get defensive or try to brush it all aside ("It's nothing really" or "It's just a personal matter"). Don't be put off. Repeat what you've seen or heard and stay true to your conversation. Even if it is a personal matter, their general presentation, their demeanour and/or their productivity is affecting the work place, so it is a matter for you to have to deal with.

4. **Refer**; naturally enough, as a manager, you are not expected to know how to solve this matter and therefore, you need to refer them onto the Employee Assistance Program for example. Alternatively, encourage them to make an appointment with their doctor or a clinical psychologist. Help them get more information about the symptoms, causes and treatment of their condition or their situation.

5. **Follow up**; As a leader you need to continue to show support. Follow up and ask how it all turned out. Keep in continued liaison with the team member on a regular basis and ensure that they are getting the help that they need and require.

Mediating between Team Members

As indicated previously, people have a habit of stepping on one another's toes and egos get put out and people often get hurt or offended. This might mean that individuals avoid each other or have little to do with each other or they might be openly sharing barbs and caustic comments or perhaps they could be indulging in gossip, rumour and innuendo.

Regardless, none of this is helpful for team dynamics and if left unchecked, can impact team morale and team culture. As the leader, this is not something that is naturally going to go away and you need to intervene.

How you do this is called **mediation**. In my experience, this is not something that needs to be referred to the HR department or to the Employee Assistance Program (EAP) because this only tends to blow it all out of proportion. You also lose control as the leader of the process and what is happening and have little idea what is going on between the team members involved. It is highly advisable that you be the mediator and stay in control.

This does not have to be unnecessarily complicated. There are particular steps as listed below that simply means that you need to have your listening skills well-tuned and you need to be able to ask good questions.

The Model for Mediation

The **purpose of mediation** is to help people who are in some sort of conflict to get to the bottom of their own problems and to help them devise their own solutions.

The **role** of the mediator (or leader) is to act as a go-between for the people in dispute. Let each person present his or her own side of the conflict. It is *not a formal process* as such. **It is an opportunity for the two parties to work out their own solutions with a third person or mediator present.** It is **not** appropriate for third parties or support persons to be present. Again, this is a mediation process where the two persons involved sort out their own situation and come to a resolution themselves about how to work together.

Mediation deals directly with the relationship between the two people in conflict. The question of right and wrong is not important. **Mediation is concerned with the future actions and behaviour of both people in dispute**. What is the best agreement that can be worked out by both people which avoids the problem once they leave mediation? How can both team members best act towards one another when they come into conflict after they leave mediation? How can they best work together? They don't have to like each other, but they do have to get on.

A key point to note, that during the mediation, when trying to get the people in conflict to come to an agreement, the **mediator or leader also helps the individuals to understand what consequences await them should they fail to reach an agreement through mediation**. Often, if the individuals involved cannot work out their own solutions to the problem, then, the organisation may intervene and bring about less desired solutions. People need to understand this.

The Steps for Mediation

Step 1: The leader meets separately with the individuals who are in conflict. Each person tells his/her story, how he/she feels about the problem and how he/she believes that the situation can be remedied or what kind of solution can be found. It is the leader's job to simply listen and understand the individual's story without taking sides, laying blame or in any way finding fault. The leader's job is to be entirely neutral and to push each person to come up with various solutions to their issues.

Step 2: The individuals concerned then return for an additional face-to-face discussion together after having met separately in the first instance. Generally speaking, this is usually only for one face-to-face meeting, but it could also be the case that additional meetings need to be held until there is a possible solution to the problem. The leader tries to help the people in conflict work out whatever misunderstanding and bad feelings they may have toward one another and how these feelings can be resolved.

Before I start this Step 2 with the two individuals concerned, I hand out my "Ground Rules" which sets the expectations for what I expect to happen in such a meeting. See **Appendix 6** for those rules. Both parties are expected to sign before the session begins. This is important, because it sets the scene for the interaction and if either staff member gets out of line in any way, then you can quite rightly point to the "rules" which they had previously agreed to and signed.

Step 3: If and when an agreement is reached by the people who are in conflict, they are brought together to write up and sign their agreement. Although the discussions are private and confidential, the final agreement is written up so that there is no misunderstanding between the two parties and so that you as the leader know how to manage each party in the light of the agreement that has been worked out.

Step 4: The leader meets with the parties to review the agreement and how it is working. This is generally a week or two later with further reviews as necessary, say, one month later and then two months later. It is important to ensure that the agreement "sticks" and that the agreed behaviours and communications are being maintained. Don't believe for a moment that simply because two individuals sign an agreement that they will demonstrate impeccable behaviour and attitude. You need to monitor the situation until you are satisfied that it is being sustained. If both parties are still happy with their progress, after say three months, then mediation is deemed to be concluded.

Chapter 12 Summary
Dealing with Conflict

There is absolutely no doubt in my mind that handling conflict is the one area that terrifies most managers and leaders. This chapter looks at a number of scenarios that might arise in the workplace and examines how to deal with them.

The Team Member Comes to You all Fired Up

There are 13 steps involved that means if you remember to follow them, then the chances are that you will successfully manage that staff member who comes to you with an issue especially if they seem tense, annoyed or visibly angry or perhaps sad or overwhelmed.

You go to the Team Member with an Issue

How do you communicate in a straightforward genuine manner without creating defensiveness or hostility from the staff member? How can you discuss with the team member in such a way that you do not intentionally offend them?

One of the most important attributes of being supportive in your communication is the ability to be *descriptive* rather than *evaluative* in the delivery of the message. In this respect, there are 7 specific steps to follow to ensure that you as the leader get your message across.

Team Member with a Mental Health Issue

How do you approach a team member whom you suspect might have a mental health issue? In my experience, most managers and leaders tend to shy away from mental health issues for a number of reasons.

The simple formula in order to assist is as follows:

Observe ⟶ *Offer Feedback* ⟶ *Listen* ⟶ *Refer* ⟶ *Follow up*

These actions have a good chance of being helpful and can prevent the problem from escalating.

Mediating between Team Members

People have a habit of stepping on one another's toes. As a result, this might mean that individuals avoid each other or have little to do with each other or they might be openly sharing barbs and caustic comments or perhaps they could be indulging in gossip, rumour and innuendo all of which impacts team morale and culture.

As a leader, the most appropriate way to intervene is to undertake a mediation process.

The Model for Mediation

The **purpose of mediation** is to help people who are in some sort of conflict to get to the bottom of their own problems and to help them devise their own solutions.

The Steps for Mediation

There are 4 Steps to this process which ends with a signed written agreement between the two parties about how to resolve their issue(s). It is important though to follow up such an agreement on a regular basis to see that the agreement has 'stuck'. Don't believe for a moment that simply because staff have agreed to certain actions in front of you as their leader, that they will be faithful to those agreements. You need to follow up, and follow up some more, not only to show staff that you mean business, but to ensure that their new behaviours and attitudes become a way of being and are being sustained over time.

CHAPTER 13

Dealing with Difficult People

The leader's job is managing people and as we well know, no two people are alike. We also know that some people who are considered steady, dependable and reliable also have their "off" days or have situations in their lives which can cause stress impacting their work performance. We also know that some people are just chronically difficult and are that way no matter what environment or setting they might be in.

It is also a truism in my experience, and in relation to your staff, that the 80:20 principle applies. Around 80% of your time and effort is usually taken up with 20% of your staff. In other words, it is that minority of employees who seem to consume most of your energy and time as a leader. It is therefore important you know how to deal with them.

Common Characteristics

As mentioned, some of your team members who are seen as stable and reliable may well be "difficult" at particular times and this could well be due to life's circumstances (eg., relationship issues, family issues, health issues, financial issues) and as such, they generally need some empathy and understanding from you and then some ways to help resolve their issues. This doesn't mean of course, that you need to fix their issue, but you simply need to give them some space with support and caring to resolve whatever is going on in their life at the time. These are typically short-term issues and can be dealt with in a relatively short time frame.

With other team members, their "condition" is more enduring and long-term and generally speaking, it may well be a case that you will need to eventually ease them out of the business because it is rare for such persons to change and they simply create poor team morale and a toxic culture. Irrespective, whether the issues are short-term for some staff or longer-term for others, they tend to involve the following:

- Unreliability
- Poor attitude
- Non-supportive behavior
- Failure to meet deadlines

- Failure to fulfil job responsibilities
- Irresponsibility
- Need for frequent retraining
- Substance or alcohol abuse

Who are the Difficult Team Members?

There are a number of particular "types" who typically cause problems in the workplace. These people are chronically difficult in that they were like this before you met them and they probably will go through life the same way. These so-called "difficult people" are well known and the ways to handle them are outlined below.

Dictator or Bully

1. How do you Recognise Them?
- Use their presence (physical & verbal) to intimidate others
- Bully & bombard
- Put others down
- Base their decisions on their personal facts now and not the facts listed in books, libraries, surveys, etc.
- Have a need to prove they're right now

2. What is their Basic Message?
- You're in my way, move over or lay down or I'll blow you away
- I count, you don't
- Give in to me and I'll pretend we get along

3. What is your typical Automatic Self-talk (and your feelings) when Confronted with a Bully?

- "What are they mad at me about now?" (Guilt, unsure, confused)
- "Why do they dislike me so much?" (Anxiety, self-doubt, hurt)
- "Who do they think they are, I'll show them!" (Annoyance, anger)
- "What can I do? If I say my peace, we've got World War 3, and if I say nothing I get trampled over." (Helplessness, powerlessness)

4. What Not to Do

- Fight (because they always win)
- Take it all personally (because they are like this with everyone)
- Give in too easily (because you'll be a target in future)
- Put yourself down
- Cry, act hurt
- Avoid them

5. What do you Actually do?

1. Stand up to them by saying things like:
    a. "In my opinion…"
    b. "In my judgment…"
    c. "I'm not sure I agree with you, but tell me more"
2. Call them by name (it equalises the conversation)

3. Feedback that they are interrupters (typically they jump in and cut you off):
   a. "Excuse me [Name], but you just interrupted me (don't say, "Don't interrupt" because it just spurs them on to a fight)
   b. Feedback that they are angry and say, "You're feeling angry because..."

Snipers

1. How do you Recognise Them?
- They are "friendly", but are critical and usually in the form of a joke (underneath it all they are angry)
- Use sarcasm, stab you with putdowns, digs, and false rumours
- They shoot from the cover of humour (cover is given to them by the victims who pretend nothing is happening and victims who may smile and laugh along with everyone else)
- Attack from behind
- Gang up before attack and try to build allies and marshall the troops

2. What is their Basic Message?
- I am very clever and skilled and I'll get you in the end
- Don't tangle with me because I'll bring you down from behind later
- I am right, but it costs too much to attack you openly

- Pretend you didn't hear me, play my game and don't make a scene publicly
- Be careful about what you say around here because I'll embarrass you in public

3. What is your typical Automatic Self-talk (and your feelings) when Confronted with a Sniper?

- "Maybe they're right, I'm not doing as well" (Self-doubt, anxiety)
- "Who in the heck is saying this stuff about me?" (Anxiety, unsure, confusion, lack of confidence)
- "Who else believes this stuff which is going around?" (Anxiety, uncertainty, insecurity)
- "What can I do to stop this? I don't know where to start?" (Helplessness, powerlessness)

4. What Not to Do

- Ignore and pretend that it didn't happen (because that's what they want)
- Agree with them
- Laugh along with them
- Wait for them to see reason and change (they will never change; this is what gives them a buzz so there's no way that they'll change)

5. What do you Actually do?
Smoke them out by saying:
1. "I thought I just heard you having a go / shot at me and I want to know, were you?" (**NB:** They will come back with one of 3 ploys):
   i. "Oh you're too sensitive"

    ii. "Can't you take a joke"

    iii. "Oh, you're too serious (or too intense)"

2. You simply come back again and repeat your first statement, "I thought I heard you having another go / shot at me again, like you did before, and I want to know, were you?" (by this time, they'll really have no-where to go and realise that their game is up; if they actually decide though to have a further dig at you, then simply continue with the repeat statement; this will destroy their game).

Know-it-all

1. How do you Recognise Them?
- Roll over you with information, facts and details
- Bombard you; they are absolutely certain they know it all
- Always have the right answer
- They don't listen; are difficult to persuade once they make a decision
- Speak with a condescending tone because they are superior

2. What is their Basic Message?
- I am right; you are wrong
- Don't disagree with me or I'll make you look stupid
- Don't take me on because I know all there is to know and I'll beat you and dump on you every time

- My mind is made up; there is no discussion

3. What is your typical Automatic Self-talk (and your feelings) when Confronted with a Know-it-all?

- "Strike, they know too much; I don't know much at all" (Self-doubt, anxiety)
- "They seem so certain that they are right, maybe I'm wrong after-all" (Uncertainty, confusion, insecurity)
- "It's no use, I can't get anywhere with them" (Despairing, helplessness, powerlessness)
- "Maybe they're right, and I'll just give in and go along" (Despondent, submission)

4. What Not to Do

- Try to be an expert yourself – it's like a red rag to a bull
- Put yourself down (because the know-it-all will agree with you)
- Try to out do them or show them up or embarrass them (they'll collect more facts and ammunition for the next round)
- Be unprepared or unsure

5. What do you Actually do?

- Simply paraphrase and feedback the main points
- Use two main question types to drill down further:

i. "I'm not sure I understand, can you explain it further?"

ii. Use "What if..." questions to spin out their ideas, plans or facts

- If necessary, go and collect further information and facts

Whiner or Complainer

1. How do you Recognise Them?
- Whine and complain about everything
- Blame others and find fault
- Tend to go on and on once they get started
- Have a tone of voice that is accusatory (because it is someone else's fault) and look at you to fix it and solve it
- Appear powerless and passive

2. What is their Basic Message?
- I'm helpless and powerless
- You are the one who can fix it (not me)
- Don't mess this up or I'll complain and whine about you too
- Be a nice person and listen to all my problems and woes

3. What is your typical Automatic Self-talk (and your feelings) when Confronted with a Whiner?

- "How come I didn't see these issues or problems?" (Self-doubt, uncertainty)
- "How can I turn them off and shut them down?" (Despair, confusion, frustration)
- "Maybe they're right, maybe the system is a problem" (Submission, giving in)
- "How come I have to fix up all these problems?" (Self-doubt, annoyance, resentment)

4. What Not to Do

- Agree, evaluate or reinforce their complaints
- Defend or apologise for yourself
- Be their "buddy" and their dumping ground
- Try to change them (you only need to cope with them)
- Let them get away without taking responsibility for any solutions

5. What do you Actually do?

1. Actively listen
2. Simply paraphrase
3. Ask questions
4. Ask for the problems in writing and keep them to deadlines
5. Learn to cut off the discussion with a statement that sets a time limit (eg., "Where do you want this discussion to be in 10 minutes time? (when I have to leave)"

6. Press for solutions which are time framed or have a deadline

Exploder or Eruptor

1. How do you Recognise Them?
- Are very nice and agreeable and then suddenly explode
- Are very scary people
- They yell, insult you and cut you down and are out of control
- Happens when you least expect it

2. What is their Basic Message?
- If I can't get my way, I'll throw a temper tantrum
- I feel vulnerable, cornered, frustrated or threatened
- Don't do this to me, back off and go away

3. What is your typical Automatic Self-talk (and your feelings) when Confronted with an Exploder?
- "What on earth is happening?" (Confusion, surprise, shock)
- "Oh wow, I must have really stuffed this up" (Self-doubt, insecurity)
- "I'm not going to take this garbage, I'll fix them!" (Anger, revenge)
- "Oh no. What do I do now?" (Confusion, anxiety)

4. What Not to do
- Get furious and fight back
- Become passive and walk out
- Walk around them like you're on egg shells
- Take their explosions personally (because they do this with lots of people)

5. What do you Actually do?
1. Do nothing – look them in the eye and wait for them to run down
2. Say in a concerned way, "I want to hear what you've got to say, but not this way"
3. Find a private place to talk
4. Get the **facts** about what actually happened
5. Offer concrete help straight away

Nay-sayer or Wet Blanket

1. How do you Recognise Them?
- They say "no" to everything
- Are generally negative
- Are cup half empty
- Find excuses not to perform or do something

2. What is their Basic Message?
- I have no power over my life
- Others can't be trusted
- Always expect the worse and then you won't be disappointed
- Don't rely on others because they'll always let you down

3. What is your Automatic Self-talk (and your feelings) when Confronted with a Nay-sayer?

- "Oh no. Here we go again" (Annoyance, frustration)
- "Maybe there's an element of truth in what they have to say" (Uncertainty, insecurity)
- "Can't they ever say anything positive?" (Annoyance, anger, resentment)

4. What Not to do

- Don't argue with them (they are too fixed in life being negative)
- Don't agree with them and take on their issues
- Don't take it personally (they are like this with everyone)

5. What do you Actually do?

1. Come back with a positive or realistic comment of your own
2. Acknowledge their point, but put your own point across ("You're probably right, but...")
3. Ask what the worst outcome might be (expose their fears and bring it out into the open)
4. Be ready to act on your own (keeps you from being dragged down by them)

Chapter 13 Summary
Dealing with Difficult People

The leader's job is managing people and as we well know, no two people are alike. We also know that some people who are considered steady and reliable also have their "off" days or have situations in their lives which can cause stress impacting their work performance. We also know that some people are just chronically difficult and are that way no matter what environment or setting or workplace they might be in.

Common Characteristics
Whether the issues are more acute or are more chronic in nature, they probably involve poor attitude or behaviour (or both).

Who are the Difficult Team Members?
These people are chronically difficult in that they were like this before you met them, and they probably will go through life the same way. These so-called "difficult people" are well known to all of us. So, how do you easily recognise them and what are the ways to handle them? These kinds of people can be categorised as follows:

Dictator or Bully
Sniper
Know-it-all
Whiner or Complainer
Exploder or Eruptor
Nay-sayer or Wet Blanket

CHAPTER 14

Being Organised: Getting Things Done

Anthony Robbins says that most people fail in life because they major in the minor things in life. So that brings me to the notion of time. What are you majoring in?

I don't know about you, but I certainly have heard myself say things like, "There's never enough time". People in all walks of life are now complaining that they are "time poor". This is especially so for leaders who are constantly trying to find some work-life balance. This so-called scarcity of time makes them feel discontent and unhappy. It's almost like people are fighting time or struggling against time or against the clock. "Where has the time gone?" they say.

However, there are 86,400 seconds in a day, 24 hours in a day, and 168 hours in a week. You are not going to get any more. That's it; end of story – 168 hours a week is what you have to play with. But we often say to ourselves things like, "When I find the time." I'm sorry, but there's no more time to "find". It's 168 hours – there's no more, no less.

Charles Buxton once said, "You will never find time for anything. If you want time you must make it". Wise words. For people who say that they don't have enough time, I remind them that they have exactly the same number of hours per day that were given to people like Helen Keller, Pasteur, Michelangelo, Mother Theresa, Leonardo da Vinci, Thomas Jefferson, Albert Einstein, and anyone else you want to name or think about. You still have only 168 hours a week, just like they had. How you use it is what matters.

"Once you have mastered time, you will understand how true it is that most people overestimate what they can accomplish in a year – and underestimate what they can achieve in a decade!"

(Anthony Robbins)

Time Wasters

So what are those things that typically get in our way and cause us to lose time. There are some common ones which seem to occur regardless of the workplace or the nature of the work. Check the list below and see if any of these are culprits within your work-life.

1. General Interruptions

This is one of the most common time robbers. You may do well to look closely at your day's routine and ask what is happening. If the interruption is necessary, then it is not a time waster. Perhaps doing a time log of activities can help you spot the costly and insignificant interruptions that might be occurring as part of your job. You might also ask yourself the following question as you are about to embark on a task, "Is this going to be the best use of my time?"

2. Meetings

Meetings seem to dominate a day's activities. How many of us have been in a meeting which lasted for an hour or more, that could have been over in about 15 minutes. And how many meetings have you been in where you came away with no real actions and you mused to yourself, "What was that all about?" The key therefore is to determine how these meetings can be run more effectively. Is there an agenda? Is the meeting chair or facilitator keeping the meeting directed and "on song". Is someone keeping track of all actions that need to be completed? Do we start the meeting knowing clearly what we want out if it?

3. Clutter

I have certainly heard people say that when their desk or workspace is cluttered, so is their brain or headspace. So, what will it take for you to have a system that allows you to have a place for everything as well as ensuring that the filing system on your computer is also neat and systematised.

"Clutter is nothing more than postponed decisions."

(Barbara Hemphill)

---

4. Lacking Goals

Having a lack of goals will also rob you of productive time because it causes you not to be focused and means you are more likely to be distracted. There is a stack of research showing that having clear goals enhances commitment, achievement and performance. There are certainly plenty of reasons for not having specific goals and sometimes it is simply a case of being too busy and overwhelmed to actually take time out to set some goals.

5. Email

We simply don't seem to be able to get away from it. It is there 24/7. Whether the emails are addressed to us personally or whether we are simply copied in, they tend to hit our Inbox with rapid regularity.

I had a coaching session with a leader recently, and as she got up to leave, she glanced down at her smartphone and sighed that during our session, she'd received 29 emails. Almost every leader I know struggles with how to manage their emails and with trying to get the balance between getting back to people while at the same time managing their team and having the appropriate amount of interpersonal interaction.

Some leaders that I am aware of have a rider at the bottom of their automated response which says something along the lines that they will only be checking emails once or twice a day and therefore the sender ought not to expect an immediate reply.

6. Poor Structure

I'm fascinated by the number of direct reports that some leaders have. Convention says it ought to be a maximum of about seven reports. If it's more than that, maybe you ought to look at your structure and see how you can put in an additional level of authority to reduce your load.

Furthermore, I'm aware that some leaders are spread too thinly and are on too many committees, working parties or projects. People in my workshops have often heard me say, "Keep the main thing, the main thing".

When you are spread too thinly, you're asking for trouble. It might be flattering to be included on a special project or your ego might get a boost about being invited, but it could be your un-doing.

Figure out what your KPIs are and what your group's strategy is going forward and be rigorous keeping to it. No apologies. No "ifs", no "buts".

Moreover, many leaders don't delegate appropriately. We've already handled that topic in Chapter 11. As we've discussed, delegation is about growing and developing your reports. After all, as the old saying goes, if you can't be replaced, you can't be promoted.

Remedies for Clawing Back Time

1. Next day planning list

Each weekday afternoon, make a list of what you have to do the next day, because if you haven't committed to your day in writing, it probably won't happen. Let me tell you very clearly, when you write things down, your brain gets it. Writing is very, very powerful.

Try to get into the habit of doing this at the end of the day. Some of my clients spend the last 10-15 minutes while they are at work to sort through their list for the next day. A few prefer to do this after dinner or just before bedtime (as long as it doesn't then keep you awake by thinking about it), but the more that you can introduce this task into a routine, the more likely it will be that you actually get things done.

2. Do your most important job first

Do your most important job first each day. Lots of people confess to being procrastinators. We kind of put things off and delay. There's a story about a steel manufacturing CEO from the United States who was given this idea by an employee (of doing the most important job first) and he was so grateful that he sent his employee a cheque for $35,000. The CEO said, "This is how much doing the most important thing first each day has saved me".

"To do two things at once is to do neither."

(Publius Syrus)

Many of us get distracted first thing in the morning for example, with our emails and perhaps Facebook or Twitter or surfing the net. The minutes go by and before we know it, a half hour has gone or even more. Yet the morning is when we are freshest and have the most energy, and hence, this is when we need to do the jobs that matter most. Emails and the like can wait.

3. Substantially reduce one time-waster each week

Your task is to try to reduce time wasting and although you'll never completely succeed in eliminating all of those time wasters in your life, you would do well to try to reduce at least some of them.

What would it take for example, for you to reduce general interruptions? Would that mean booking an interview room where you can work on a report in peace and quiet? What would it take to look at ways in which meetings can be shortened and more productive?

4. Spend your time as though you had to buy it

Think about that for a moment. Before you spend an hour or more reading a report or going to a particular meeting, ask yourself, "Would I spend my own money to do this?" If you look at your time as a financial investment and see how you spend it, you might make more prudent decisions about how you are spending time.

5. Batch routine jobs

Most people complain about some of the biggest times wasters being social media or responding to emails.

For these kinds of tasks, it is important to have a batching routine by carving out specific times in the day for such tasks and then communicating this routine to recipients and others. For example, with emails, you can employ an auto-responder message which says something like, *"Thank you for you message, but I only check emails twice a day at 11.00am and 4.00pm on weekdays. If the matter is urgent, please phone ...... on ....".*

This means that you're not then distracted through the day with those constant emails, and people know what your procedure is, and you also give them an avenue if the issue is urgent.

"Our life is frittered away by detail...simplify, simplify."

(Henry David Thoreau)

---

6. Reduce distractions

We all have them, and these distractions all seem to vie for our attention. What can you do to eliminate these or reduce their impact? The best time managers will turn off their social media notifications, close down all unnecessary tabs on their computer and put their phone on airplane or flight mode.

Some bring in noise-cancelling head-phones into the office which are especially helpful in an open-plan office. Of course, you can always close your door (and even put a sign on it to say do not disturb – or words to that effect) or else book out an interview room to yourself to ensure some solitude while you work on an important matter. It's vital to do all you can to remove as many distractions as you can to assist you to concentrate and focus on what is in hand.

7. Keep Meetings Under 15 Minutes

A tip for running meetings; circulate the agenda beforehand and conduct the meeting standing up. It's a great way to get through meetings! I left a job at a hospital some time back because of what John Cleese calls in his original training film *Meetings, Bloody Meetings.* There were so many meetings. All those meetings finally got to me. I used to sit in the meetings and calculate the amount of money being wasted in wages for the sake of people just talking to hear themselves talk. I wish I'd known this rule back then!

I coach a principal in a pathology company and each morning they have a 10-15 minute stand up meeting around the kitchen table in the staff room. Everyone gets a sense about what is happening for the day and can report on the activities of the previous day.

Similarly, there is a young man I coach who is a fitter and turner by trade and he has instituted "tool box" meetings each morning where the workers stand around in a group to be briefed on what's on for the day and the day's priorities; it takes no longer than 10 minutes. He says it's invaluable in that it's short, employees know what is going on and it has cut down the mistakes that are made in the factory.

Maybe think about daily meetings, but 15 minutes at a time.

8. Maximum of 4 meetings in a day with gaps

If you are not able to limit your meetings to 15 minutes, then one of the most effective recipes for managing time that I have worked out with executives and leaders is this; limit yourself to a maximum of four meetings in a day, but more importantly, **ensure that there is at least a half-hour gap between meetings**.

If you really want to stress yourself and be ragged at the end of the day, then try for back-to-back meetings and cram the day with them. It is a sure-fire way to drain your energies quickly and to make sure that you become non-productive and ineffective.

I've seen it countless times.

The meetings are back-to-back, but they always seem to run over time. The leader is immediately stressed because the meeting has gone over and then arrives late to the next meeting without any time to collect their thoughts or get prepared. They arrive at the next meeting and due to the fluster of getting there late, it takes them 10 to 15 minutes to get their head right to participate in the present meeting. Of course too, they may well have had actions from the previous meeting which are now mounting up and will be added to the actions from the present meeting.

You can see how this mounts up and by the end of the day, the leader is completely frazzled or "fried".

9. Spend up to 30 minutes a day thinking

Someone once said, "Thinking is the hardest work there is, which is probably why so few engage in it!"

Those who spend time actually thinking for at least 15 minutes a day (and preferably 30 minutes) have an edge on others because they've done their homework beforehand, and have life a bit more in perspective.

This is actually what effective leaders do, and we all are our own personal leaders. (See below regarding Quadrant 2 as described by Dr. Stephen Covey.)

I've coached a number of leaders and individuals who have lamented that they don't have enough time to be able to sit and plan and think! Failure to do so inevitably means that you are handling more crises and putting out more fires than you need to do.

Maybe you won't put aside time on a daily basis, but what about weekly?

I've coached a CEO for example, who has decided that each Thursday she will go into the office in the morning and then around 10.30am tell people that she was going out. She'd take the lift to the ground floor and walk around the corner to a coffee shop where she'd sit and think and plan for the next hour at least. I coached an architect who would each Friday morning tell his executive assistant that he was going out for a meeting and then go to the State Library for two hours with his laptop, and his i-pad to think, plan and strategise.

Put aside time to think. It directly helps in being able to control your life and get life more in balance.

Time in Four Boxes

You may be familiar with Dr. Stephen Covey, a popular author, who wrote *The 7 Habits of Highly Effective People.* (If you haven't read that book, put it on your "to read" list; it's been a best seller for over 25 years.) In that book, Covey said that there are two ways to really understand **time,** or two dimensions to time, namely, that which is **urgent** and that which is **important**.

In other words, he said you can think about things being urgent and not urgent, and there are things that are important and not important in regards to time.

It's an interesting concept in which to think about time and it gives a very interesting perspective that most people find helpful once it has been explained.

According to your diary, your
schedule is the same as always . . .
9:00 am: Arrive at work.
9:05 am: Let the chaos ensue.

He said that when you divide time up into those two categories, you get some enlightening patterns developing.

You actually get four quadrants (see the table below).

	Urgent	**Not Urgent**
Important	**I** • Crises • Pressing Problems • Deadline-driven projects, meetings, preparations	**II** • Preparation • Prevention • Values clarification • Planning • Relationship building • True re-creation • Empowerment
Not Important	**III** • Interruptions, some phone calls • Some mail, email, some reports • Some meetings • Many proximate, pressing matters • Many popular activities	**IV** • Trivia, busywork • Junk mail • Some phone calls • Internet surfing • Facebook, Twitter • Social media • Time wasters • "Escape" activities

In the **first quadrant**, you have things that are **both** *urgent* and *important*. These include crises, pressing problems, projects, and meetings that are deadline driven. This is the **Fire-fighting Quadrant**. This is where most people tend to live their day, especially in the work environment. Live all of your life in this quadrant though, and you become stressed, you become anxious and/or depressed and/or grumpy, irritable and angry, and sadly, you eventually burn out.

"Careful planning puts you ahead in the long run; hurry and scurry puts you further behind."

(Proverbs 21:5)

Going down the table is the **third quadrant** where things are also *urgent*, but **not** *important*. They might look important, but they really are not. Covey calls this the **Quadrant of Deception**. These include interruptions, some phone calls, some mail, some emails, some reports, some meetings – they may look like they are pressing matters, but they're not really. We tend to lose a good deal of time in this quadrant focusing on things that feign importance, but are not really important. In a sense, we get conned and distracted by the unimportant.

Then there is the **second quadrant,** in which matters are **not** *urgent*, but they are *important*. This is the

Quality Time Quadrant. This is where you have to prepare things. You need to plan, prepare, create, think about things and work things out. This is where you take time out. You organise things, prioritise and set things in order. You work out what's important to do and what you value. You might manage risk and determine a Plan A and a possible Plan B for a situation.

Finally, in **quadrant four**, things are **not** *urgent* and they are **not** *important*. This is the **Escape Quadrant**. In this quadrant are things like trivia, social media, and junk mail, and some phone calls.

This is when people stand at the photocopier or the water-cooler and gossip at work, or surf the internet, or hang over the fence at home and talk about nothing or turn on the television and "veg out". In other words, they are time wasters, and Covey argues that if you live all your life in Quadrant one, in the crises, then to relieve the pressure and to escape, you have to move down to Quadrant four with the trivia. If you spend too much time in this Quadrant at work, then, you guessed it, you get fired.

"There is never enough time to do everything, but there is always enough time to do the most important thing."

(Brian Tracy)

Good Use of Time

Now let me ask you two questions. **What is the one activity that you know would have a significant positive impact on your *personal life* if you did it superbly well and consistently?**

What is the one activity that you know would have a significant positive impact on your *career* if you did it superbly well and consistently?

Think about these two questions. How would you answer them? Take a few minutes and write down your responses.

Let me suggest that your answers would typically fall into one of seven categories, namely:
 ➢ Improving communication
 ➢ Better planning and organising
 ➢ Taking better care of yourself
 ➢ Seizing the opportunity
 ➢ Better preparation
 ➢ Personal development
 ➢ Empowerment

If your answers did fall into one of these seven categories, then let me ask a further question.

In which quadrant do these activities fall?

Answer: *Quadrant two*. Quadrant two is important, but not urgent. That's where we do our preparation, our planning, our thinking. So, if all of those activities are in quadrant two, and they are important, why aren't you doing them?

More particularly, what would it take for you to invest more time in those Quadrant two activities? Remember, these activities will have a significant positive impact on your personal and professional life. So, how would you organise yourself to get some Quadrant two time? What would it take for you to schedule some regular planning time? What is stopping you from getting some creative thinking time? How could you get around those obstacles?

Finding Quadrant two time gives people more control over their lives, gives them a sense of accomplishment, refreshes them, lifts their spirits, and re-energises them. Managing time and managing yourself in this way is a key to reducing your stress levels. Isn't it worth doing?

I used to coach a partner in a law firm who would drive into the city each day, but enroute, he would pull into a park overlooking lawns and gardens and spend 20 minutes thinking and planning his day. As it happens, he also did that on the way home so that he could get his head clear and not arrive home a "grumpy old man". I also coached a director in a service company who, on the drive to work, would call into his special café for an early morning coffee for at least an hour or more to think and plan.

Where would you go for your planning time? How often and when would you go? How would you work it into your daily routine? How would you remember to fit it into your schedule? What would need to happen so that it became a habit?

"Half our life is spent trying to find something to do with the time we have rushed through life trying to save."

(Will Rogers)

Chapter 14 Summary
Being Organised: Getting Things Done

Time Wasters
They are well known to most of us, but let's clearly name
the worst offenders:
1. General Interruptions
2. Meetings
3. Clutter
4. Lacking Goals
5. Email
6. Poor Structure

Remedies for Clawing Back time
So what are the ways that we can reclaim some of that
valuable lost time?
1. Next day planning list
2. Do your most important job first
3. Substantially reduce one time-waster each week
4. Spend your time as though you had to buy it
5. Batch routine jobs
6. Reduce distractions
7. Keep meetings under 15 minutes
8. Maximum of 4 meetings in a day with gaps
9. Spend up to 30 minutes a day thinking

Time in 4 Boxes
Dr Stephen Covey said that there are two ways to really
understand **time,** or two dimensions to time, namely, that
which is **urgent** and that which is **important**. When you

divide time up into those two categories, you get some interesting patterns developing. You get four quadrants where you get to understand what you are doing with your time and can attempt to control time more effectively.

It is easy for an inexperienced manager to spend too much time putting out fires and meeting obligations. Then, when the manager must get away from these pressures to survive and keep a balance, they can fritter away time on trivial pursuits. No wonder there's never enough time to do the things that are really important.

Instead, we need time to think, plan, build relationships, take care of ourselves, learn, and improve ourselves, and prioritising our time to be able to do these things will contribute greatly to our productivity and our sense of satisfaction. Failure to use time wisely is a recipe for frustration and discontent. Success comes from mastering time rather than letting it master you.

"One thing that you can't recycle is wasted time."

(Author unknown)

CHAPTER 15

The Final Word

The fact that you have read to this point in the book indicates that you seem motivated to do something about being a better leader. Good job on getting to this point.

I really like the saying that you can't change the direction of the wind, but you can adjust your sails; yes, you can make adjustments.

I like the notion that although it is difficult to suddenly arrive at your destination, you can at least change your direction and head towards where you want to go. And it's **not** about getting there in a hurry, it's about getting there enjoyably, having the choice to change direction when you want to, taking a different tack, and taking it one step at a time.

"Step by step, day by day, achievers do what non-achievers don't bother to do."

(Author unknown)

Discipline

Needless to say, all of this is going to need some **discipline**. Discipline. Yes, some people call this a "dirty" word, but Jim Rohn once said that *"Discipline is the bridge between goals and accomplishments"*.

You need to make it happen. This is exactly where so many give up and the minority succeed. This is where the few put in the effort and the majority sit back and do nothing or worse still, complain, blame and make excuses. Then when the minority make it, the majority say things like, "Aren't they lucky!" Luck? You make your own "luck" by putting in the effort. As the famous golfer Gary Player once said, "the harder I work, the luckier I get".

There is in this world, a gap between the "**knowing**" and the "**doing**". In other words, lots of the population know what to do, but do they actually do it? Indeed, it is a mark of the successful person that they bridge the gap between what they know ought to be done and actually following through. They actually do things. They actually get up and make it happen. They may not feel like doing it, but they go ahead and do it anyway. If I waited until I "felt" like going down to the gym to workout, I'd never go.

The hallmark of the successful person and leader, is that they just go and do it anyway.

"Great things are not done by impulse but by a series of small things brought together."

(Vincent van Gogh)

It's the same in business too. There are the training programs and the strategies that might be provided and outlined, but the implementation falls over. There is no follow through. No execution. What a waste of time and effort. What a way to damper morale.

Talk is cheap. You know that as well as I do. It's easy to talk. We're good at it. However, **life rewards action, not good intentions** as I've alluded to elsewhere. This is where the rubber really hits the road. This is where the men and women step up, while the boys and girls slip away.

So what is the one thing that you will take away from reading this book? What will you do differently tomorrow? But how will you do it? What is your next step? Is it making a phone call? Actually sitting down and making a plan? As a personal leader, what area are you going to start on? Maybe you've started already, so how will you stick to the task in hand?

More particularly, **how** will you remember to do these next steps? What visual prompts or reminders will you put in place to actually get started? Having a good intention will not do it. You'll forget and you'll get distracted by the busy-ness of life. And besides, your old habits will kick in and you'll be a slave to your previous routine.

Instead, help your brain out by getting a visual prompt. A client of mine had post-it notes on their mirror in the bathroom to constantly keep things in focus. Another client bought a new pen which acted as his prompt to do things differently. Still another bought a new watch band. You'll need a visual prompt to remind you about the ways that you are working to be a better leader.

Further, **who** will keep you accountable on this next step and the steps beyond? Will it be a friend? Will you hire a coach? How often will you meet to "report in"? It's easier for me to get down to the gym if I know that my personal trainer is there waiting for me. You need someone to keep you accountable. Successful people almost always have a mentor, coach or trusted ally. Who will it be for you? What is your next step to make this happen? A phone call, an email, a conversation?

"You cannot change your destination overnight, but you can change your direction overnight."

(Jim Rohn)

You owe it to yourself to be on the journey towards being the kind of leader that you want to become. You're worth it.

Chapter 15 Summary
The Final Word

Discipline
As the saying goes, "If it's going to be, it's up to me". This book might give you some important information, but it's critical not to fall into the "knowing – doing" gap.

In other words, lots of the population know what to do, but do they actually do it? Indeed, it is a mark of the successful person that they bridge the gap between what they know ought to be done and actually following through. They actually do things. They actually get up and make it happen.

You might know what to do, but what's it going to take to actually do it? Life rewards actions not good intentions.

APPENDIX 1

Governing Values

What's really important in my life?
What are the highest priorities in my life?
Of these priorities, which do I value most?

HOW TO CHOOSE YOUR TOP 5 VALUES

1. Love / Connection
2. Financial security
3. Health & fitness
4. Peace of mind / Inner harmony
5. Recognition / Appreciation
6. Respect
7. Spirituality / Relationship with God
8. Accomplishment / Achievement
9. Integrity & Honesty
10. Caring / Service
11. Education & Academics
12. Self-respect
13. Taking responsibility
14. Exercising leadership
15. Discovery / Curiosity
16. Intelligence
17. Sense of Purpose
18. Happiness / Positive Attitude
19. Making a Contribution / Legacy
20. Quality of life
21. Perspective / Wisdom
22. Adventure
23. Resilience
24. Self-control
25. Ambition
26. Imagination & Creativity
27. Forgiveness
28. Generosity
29. Friendship
30. Appreciation of Beauty
31. Courage
32. Loyalty
33. Dependable / Reliable
34. Independence / Autonomy
35. Empathy & Understanding

36. Fun / Enjoyment   38.   ....

37. Personal growth /
    Learning

The following questions may help you to identify even more of the values that are most important in your life:

- What are all the qualities that make your life better?
- What helps you to survive, thrive and prosper?
- What would you miss it if were eliminated from your life?
- What qualities define the person you want to be?

Start with choosing your top **ten values**. Don't worry about the order. Just put them down as you think about each one. Consider what's really important to you.

Value

1. ....   6. ....

2. ....   7. ....

3. ....   8. ....

4. ....   9. ....

5. ....   10. ....

Now condense your list down to 5 – your **5 core values**. What's the most important, then what's next, etc. Write them down in order and see them clearly displayed.

Order Rank   Value

1. ....

2. ....

3. ....

4. ....

5. ....

This is your **values list**. Keep it as your "ready reckoner" for reference.

These values will also help you to work out your **personal mission statement**. They act as your lighthouses to guide your life's journey, and on a daily basis, they act as guides to organise your day's priorities.

APPENDIX 2
Work Values

What a person considers worthwhile and rewarding in work influences his/her personal and career development, as well as his/her career choice.

This list looks at the kinds of work attitudes or values that you hold in relation to different aspects of work (eg., secure work, creative work, etc). It examines the kinds of features that are important to you within a job.

Importantly, these **values give you job satisfaction.** They are critical to **motivating** you towards work and keeping you engaged at work.

Review the list of 14 values. They are currently listed in alphabetical order. Select the top 5 which you consider are important to you in a job, regardless of the kind of job it might be.

Rank	Value	Description
	Challenge & Stimulation	Developing and expanding your skills and abilities at work
	Creativity	Making or doing something original through work
	Helping Others	Caring for others and attending to their needs

	Independence	Free from being told what to do at work
	Influence of Work	Wanting to be free from having to work in your spare time; work-life balance
	Job Security	Wanting a secure job and remaining employable
	Managing Others	Wanting to be in charge of other workers
	Organisation	Following a systematic, routine and scheduled approach to work
	Own Life Style	Living where you want and not having it determined by work
	Physical Activity	To move around and be mobile at work
	Salary	Wanting large amounts of money as the reward for hard work
	Status	Wanting people to think that your work is important
	Variety	Doing different things with regular changes at work
	Working Alongside Others	Working with people who are friendly and understanding

After reviewing the list of 14 values and choosing the top 5, follow the points below.

Ask yourself, "Am I happy with the top 3 to 5 values?" If not, what would you move out of the top list and what would you move into this top set of values?

Now ask yourself, "What is a must for me? What values are non-negotiable? Which values must I have in a job or career?"

These values are your guide for job satisfaction.

List your top "must have" values here followed by those that would be "nice to have":

1. ....

2. ....

3. ....

4. ....

5. ....

Keep these values in focus.
They are your guide to job satisfaction.

246

APPENDIX 3

Your Eulogy

Now take a few minutes to jot down your impressions, your thoughts. How do you want to be seen or remembered? What's important to you? What things would you like people to say about you? Jot down points. Let the pen flow. Don't censor. Just write. Just keep writing, don't think; just write. Just try to capture thoughts at this stage.

....

....

....

....

....

....

....

....

....

....

....

....

....

....

....
....
....
....
....
....
....
....
....
....
....
....
....
....
....

Now consider **your own eulogy.** What do you want your eulogy to consist of? What would matter most at the end of your life? What do you want to be remembered for? Write it out in full. Be proud of it. Own it.

APPENDIX 4

Johari Window Exercise
for Self-awareness

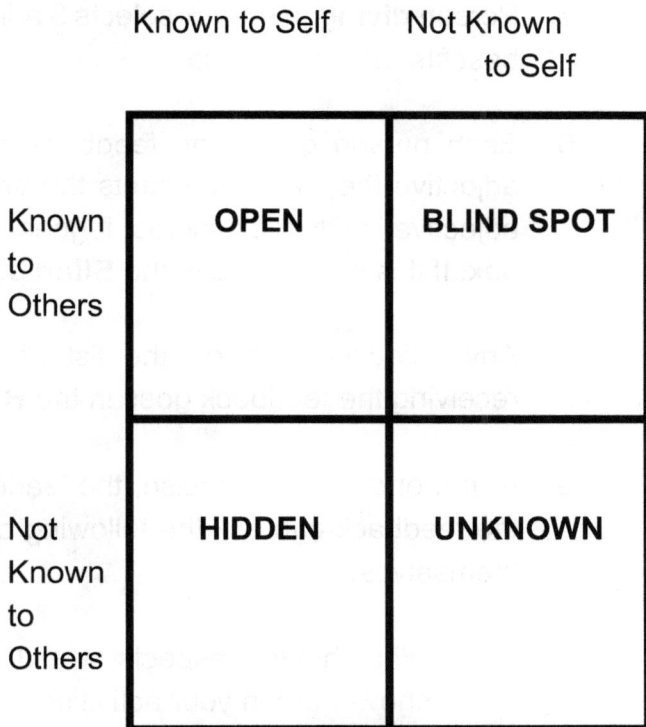

	Known to Self	Not Known to Self
Known to Others	OPEN	BLIND SPOT
Not Known to Others	HIDDEN	UNKNOWN

(The Johari Window, Luft, 1969)

1. Find a trusted work colleague or peer either from your current place of work or possibly a previous place of work.

2. Draw up the grid as shown above on a piece of blank paper.

3. Review the list of the adjectives provided on the page below.

4. Person **receiving** feedback chooses 12 adjectives that represents them.

5. Person **giving** feedback selects 8 adjectives that best fits the other person.

6. Each person giving the feedback reveals one adjective they feel represents the person. If the adjective is ON their list too, it goes in the **Open** box. If it is not, it goes in the **Blind** box.

7. Any adjectives left on the list of the person receiving the feedback goes in the **Hidden** box.

8. At the end of this exercise, the leader receiving the feedback can ask the following questions of themselves:

   a. What hidden aspects would you like to show more in your activities as a leader?
   b. How can you maximise or minimise your blind spots?
   c. What was your key insight?

Johari Window Adjectives

Your Name: …………………………………..

Date: ……………………….

| **For Partner** | | **For You** | |
Circle 8 Objectives		Circle 12 Objectives	
Able	Mature	Able	Mature
Accepting	Modest	Accepting	Modest
Adaptable	Nervous	Adaptable	Nervous
Bold	Observant	Bold	Observant
Brave	Organised	Brave	Organised
Calm	Patient	Calm	Patient
Caring	Powerful	Caring	Powerful
Cheerful	Proud	Cheerful	Proud
Clever	Quiet	Clever	Quiet
Complex	Reflective	Complex	Reflective
Confident	Relaxed	Confident	Relaxed
Dependable	Religious	Dependable	Religious
Dignified	Responsive	Dignified	Responsive
Energetic	Searching	Energetic	Searching
Extroverted	Self-assertive	Extroverted	Self-assertive
Friendly	Self-conscious	Friendly	Self-conscious
Giving	Sensible	Giving	Sensible
Happy	Sentimental	Happy	Sentimental
Helpful	Shy	Helpful	Shy
Idealistic	Silly	Idealistic	Silly
Independent	Smart	Independent	Smart
Ingenious	Spontaneous	Ingenious	Spontaneous
Intelligent	Sympathetic	Intelligent	Sympathetic
Introverted	Tense	Introverted	Tense
Kind	Trustworthy	Kind	Trustworthy
Knowledgeable	Warm	Knowledgeable	Warm
Logical	Wise	Logical	Wise
Loving	Witty	Loving	Witty

APPENDIX 5

Preparing an Issue for Discussion

Preparing your presentation of an issue helps prevent incoherent or incomplete explanations of the problem. Additionally, your team members appreciate good use of their time. At the top of the list is the accurate identification of the problem.

The Issue is:

Be concise. In one or two sentences, get to the heart of the problem. Is it a concern, challenge, opportunity, or recurring problem that is becoming more troublesome?

It Is Significant Because:

What's at stake? How does this affect dollars, income, people, products, services, customers, family, timing, the future, or other relevant factors? What is the future impact if the issue is not resolved?

My Ideal Outcome Is:

What specific *results do I want?*

Relevant Background Information:

Summarize with bulleted points: How, when, why, and where did the issue start? Who are the key players? Which forces are at work? What is the issue's current status?

What I Have Done Up To This Point:

What have I done so far? What options am I considering?

The Help I Want From The Group (or Individual) Is:

What result do I want from the group (or person)? For example, alternative solutions, confidence regarding the right decision, identification of consequences, where to find more information, critique of the current plan.

APPENDIX 6

GROUND RULES FOR THE RESOLUTION OF ISSUES

1. Commit to stay until the end of the session.

2. One person at a time to speak; allow others to complete what they are saying without interruption.

3. No personal attacks.

4. No blaming; you are responsible for your own thoughts, feelings and actions or behaviours.

5. Use "I" statements, no "You" statements (eg., "I feel that...." "The way I see it is...." "The situation seems to indicate to me that...."

6. Respect any confidentiality agreement that is made (except where it is agreed that the outcome/result needs to be communicated to a nominated other party).

7. Only make commitments that you will keep.

8. Be willing to participate and to explore ways to resolve problems; come up with solutions.

*Please note that mediation is strictly a **confidential exercise**. Matters that are discussed within the confines of the mediation sessions remain within that context. Only a final public document (if one is produced) about how the parties work together will be released to the line manager or supervisor – all other information is strictly confidential.*

Signed: .... Date:.....................

Print Name:...

ABOUT THE AUTHOR

Dr Darryl Cross

- *Fellow, Australian Psychological Society*
- *Fellow, Institute of Managers and Leaders*
- *Graduate Member, Australian Institute of Company Directors*
- *Certified Personal & Executive Coach, College of Executive Coaching*
- *Certified Mentor Coach, College of Executive Coaching*
- *Member, ICF Professional Coaches*
- *Member, Institute of Coaching*
- *Accredited Facilitator, Mindshop Australia*
- *Accredited Advisor, Family Business Australia*
- *Foreign Affiliate, American Psychological Association*
- *Registered Psychologist*

Dr Darryl is a clinical and organisational psychologist as well as an internationally accredited personal and executive coach. He is an author, international speaker and guest university lecturer.

- For **executives and senior managers**, this might mean a focus on effective leadership, dealing with difficult staff, increasing productivity, succession planning, culture issues and growing the business.
- For those with **business concerns**, it might mean work-life balance, team dynamics, career progression, job dissatisfaction or dealing with conflict.
- For groups of **managers and leaders**, it would mean providing a coach training program in order to grow and develop their people.
- For **family businesses**, it would mean working out succession planning and any conflict with special attention to communication and relationships and organising a family charter.
- For **career concerns**, it might mean gaining career guidance and direction or coaching on how to gain the next promotion.
- For those with **personal concerns**, it may include lack of direction, lack of confidence or relational issues.

He has coached clients all around the globe including most parts of Australia as well as England, Ireland, the USA, Canada, Malaysia and Dubai.

> **Academic training in psychology and specific training in coaching together with life experience, means that Darryl has come up with practical ways to use life principles that work. He has the knack of being able to say it all simply.**

For more information on Dr Darryl Cross, please go to his two main websites:

www.DrDarryl.com

www.LeadershipCoaching.com.au